AULD
FOES

AULD
FOES

**World Football's
Oldest Rivalry**

James Stephen

First published by Pitch Publishing, 2023
Reprinted 2024
2

Pitch Publishing
9 Donnington Park,
85 Birdham Road,
Chichester,
West Sussex,
PO20 7AJ
www.pitchpublishing.co.uk
info@pitchpublishing.co.uk

A CIP catalogue record is available for this book
from the British Library.

ISBN 978 1 80150 508 6

Typesetting and origination by Pitch Publishing

Printed and bound in India by Replika Press Pvt. Ltd.

CONTENTS

In loving memory of Steven Ellis
Hearts supporter, and best pal

WHAT'S IN A NAME?

HIBERNIAN FOOTBALL Club were founded in 1875 and are usually referred to by one of their nicknames. Most commonly it is Hibs, but other nicknames, such as the Hi-bees or Hibees ('hi' as in high) or the Hibbies ('hi' as in him or his), are common and perfectly acceptable. The club are also sometimes known as 'the cabbage', which comes from the rhyming slang cabbage & ribs. While this is not particularly common, it is not unknown and, in fact, a popular (but now defunct) Hibernian pub was called the Cabbage & Ribs. In earlier decades, they were known variously as Hibernians, the Hibernians, the Irishmen or the Green Jerseys.

While a supporter of Hibernian could correctly be called a Hibernian, it is not common. Supporters of the club are generally referred to as a Hibee, a Hibby or Hibs daft.

The club's shorthand initials, as denoted in millions of pieces of graffiti and on the covers of thousands of school workbooks over the years, are HFC.

Hibernian as an adjective means 'of or relating to Ireland or its inhabitants' and as a noun means 'a native or inhabitant of Ireland'. This gives a good idea of why the name was chosen for the club, which sprang from the immigrant Irish community of Edinburgh. They were often referred to as the Hibernians (literally translating as the Irishmen). The club's motto, quietly dropped at an indeterminate time, was Erin Go Bragh – Irish Gaelic for Ireland Forever, which can still be seen written on scarves and flags, but not on official club merchandise.

The founding year of Heart of Midlothian Football Club is the subject of some debate, with some – including Tom Purdie, the club's first captain – claiming the club were formed in 1873. Their first recorded matches took place in 1875, when the club were also SFA members, and so it is assumed that the Heart of Midlothian Football Club came into existence not later than the autumn of 1874, a view around which the club was happy to coalesce (even if Purdie continued to disagree). The reason for this confusion could be that the original 1873 version of Heart of Midlothian to which Purdie had belonged had indeed existed, but had disbanded due to a defeat by the St Andrew's club. Three members of the disbanded Hearts then asked to join St Andrew's, and at a committee meeting they convinced the St Andrew's committee to adopt Heart of Midlothian as a distinctly Edinburgh name (and not to be confused with St Andrew's, the famous town in Fife).

Heart of Midlothian are mostly known by their nickname, Hearts. It is also correct, if less common, to refer to them by one of two other nicknames, the Jam Tarts or the Jambos. Jam Tarts is rhyming slang for Hearts, and Jambos seems to have evolved as a derivative of this in recent years.

A supporter of Hearts would most commonly be referred to as a Jambo, or simply as a Hearts man.

In initials, Hearts are denoted by HMFC. Oftentimes, the 'M' is inserted into the 'HFC' graffiti of their city rivals, usually giving them the last word in the graffiti rivalry.

Just as the founding year of the club is shrouded in myth, so too are the exact origins of the name. One story is that Hearts are named after a 19th-century dance club that was based in the Old Town of Edinburgh. Some young men who frequented it formed the football club, and named it after their favourite dance hall. Another is that a group of boys who played football around the Old Town formed a club and named it after the local landmark. Regardless of how those founding fathers chose the name, what is not in doubt is that the name Heart of Midlothian refers to the Old Tolbooth of Edinburgh (the jail) that once stood on the Royal Mile, directly outside St Giles' Cathedral and which was known as the Heart of Midlothian. The moniker was made famous by the great Edinburgh writer Sir Walter Scott and his eponymous novel. The Old Tolbooth building is long demolished, but its site is marked by a stone mosaic on the ground, in the shape of a heart (literally the Heart of Midlothian). Hearts' club crest is a replica of the mosaic.

Spitting on the actual Heart of Midlothian mosaic for good luck is a tradition still observed by some Edinburgh residents (in a throwback to the site's time as the jail). It has nothing whatsoever to do with football rivalry and is often viewed with some curiosity by the throngs of tourists on the Royal Mile. I daresay, however, that a few Hibernian fans have participated in the tradition with a tad more gusto than was necessary.

It is one of the curiosities of the Edinburgh Derby that neither of the two protagonists bears the name of their home city, or even of a district within the city, although Midlothian is the county in which Edinburgh used to be situated (the City of Edinburgh has since become its own council area). It is a minor point, but it is worth noting, not least because it does give a sense of just how parochial football was in those early years. After all, a club that was a member of and played in the Edinburgh Football Association had no more need of Edinburgh in its title than a team currently playing in the Scottish league would have for Scotland to be in its title – something that is borne out by just how few of the clubs from those early years did have any geographical signifier in their name. Leith Athletic were perhaps the most prominent, but of course Leith was very much a separate town and administrative council area in those days. Other early front-runners in Edinburgh football had such poetic names as St Bernard's (named after a famous monumental well that is in turn named for a 12th-century crusader, St Bernard of Clairvaux, in the Stockbridge area of the city), Hanover, Edina, St James's, Northern, Mossend Swifts, Waverley, Caledonian, Brunswick, Zebras, Rose, Harp, Trafalgar, Muirhouse Rovers, Edinburgh University and the first of them all, 3rd Edinburgh Rifle Volunteers.

ACKNOWLEDGEMENTS

FIRSTLY TO Pitch Publishing, who liked my idea and agreed to take it on. It's no exaggeration to say that without them, this book wouldn't be here; and to Andrea Dunn for editing the manuscript.

To the dozens and dozens of people with whom I have shared conversations about Edinburgh football, who are too numerous to mention. This book is in many ways a result of more than four decades of such conversations, soaking in what football meant, and means, to the good folk of Edinburgh.

Particularly to Ross McEwan, a big Hearts man and a good mate, for his help and insights. And for sitting on the steps of Barclay Church in a deserted Tollcross on an early summer's evening in 2020, with the haar rolling in, having a Covid lockdown carry-out beer from a plastic carton, chatting about football and encouraging me with this book before taking me on an impromptu Hearts walking tour.

To Paul Higgins and Neil Fenwick, both of whom contributed hugely, and who I can still count as among my best mates in the world, in spite of them having known me since my early teens. To Stuart Maclaren, Iain, Graeme and Murray Gillespie, Mikey McDermott, Paul, Stevie and Kenny Reid, Dad, Ants, Terry and Mark Small and all the boys, John Heron, Charlie Smith, Tony Mullen and Mark Ferguson, all of whom have shared insights, stories and anecdotes with me that are reflected in here at various points. And to Michelle, Brodie and Lawrie for listening to me droning on, and giving me the time.

Andy Mitchell, the football historian whose encyclopaedic knowledge of early Edinburgh and Scottish football was incredibly useful, and who was generous with both his time and his insight. And to the other, usually amateur, historians of Edinburgh and Scottish football whose research and insights were so valuable, particularly Brian Mark, George H. Park, Robin Holmes (whose book on former Scottish league clubs runs to an astonishing 800 pages), Alan Lugton, Tom Purdie, Craig Watson and Mike Smith. To Mark Donaldson for taking me to my first press conference at Riccarton while on work experience, and being so generous with his time.

And lastly, to Steven Ellis, my best pal at high school, and his dad Bobby. Steven and I once interviewed no less a figure than John Robertson in the Tynecastle changing rooms for a school project, and Steven and Bobby took me to my first ever Hearts match at Tynecastle, versus Partick Thistle, the score of which I have long since forgotten; but I haven't forgotten going with them.

CHAPTER 1

INTRODUCTION

'A football team represents a way of being, a culture.'

Michel Platini

'Sport is an unfailing cause of ill-will.'

George Orwell

ONE DAY at work, I was chatting to a colleague who I had never met before, who had travelled up from London for a meeting. As I often do, I steered the conversation away from work and on to football. I often wonder how much harder it would be to meet and form relationships with other men without the universal language of football; and I admit that a slight disappointment always jumps up within me if the person I am speaking to says they don't follow football (or worse, pretends they do, before making it very apparent that they really don't).

They guy I was speaking to was a real football fan though. He followed Oxford United, not one of English football's more glamorous clubs, and he took the same interest and delight at moving the conversation on to football as I did. It was during this conversation that he asked me about the Edinburgh Derby, but to my surprise, he asked if the rivalry between Heart of Midlothian and Hibernian was a *proper rivalry*. I was shocked by the question. I was shocked that a football fan such as he did not know that *of course* it was a *proper rivalry*; it was very much a *proper rivalry*.

My offence was not with him; English people rarely know or care about Scottish football, and even those with a cursory knowledge rarely look beyond the Old Firm. This is understandable, and I am guilty of the same. Most of us don't see past the big, famous rivalries in most other football countries. Ultimately, football fans are consumed by the club they support, then by their rivals, and then by the league around them. They may also pay attention to the bigger clubs in their own country or to some of the bigger clubs in other European countries, but that is usually it (unless you grew up in the 1990s, and had the ground-breaking delight of *Gazzetta Football Italia* on a Saturday morning, in which case you probably still maintain a passing interest in the Italian league).

This realisation – that a proper football fan could ask me such a question about the Edinburgh Derby – sent me into a spiral of existential angst. Is this city, and its two biggest clubs, that have played such an enormous and formative role in my life, really so irrelevant to the wider football world? How can it be that something so all-consuming to so many tens of thousands of Edinburghers can fly so far under the radar of other fans? How can it be that the second-biggest rivalry in a country so integral to the development of football is so unrecognised?

In a new book, *Divided Cities*, author Kevin Pogorzelski travels the world attending some of the great single-city derbies. The list is familiar: Rome, Old Firm, Rio, Buenos Aires; and there are some others that are slightly more left field: Lisbon, Belgrade, Seville and Genoa. 'How someone defines the finest or their favourite is such a personal vs subjective thing,' Pogorzelski explains. 'We all have different perspectives and features we look for when we categorise our own greatest list, such as importance (deciding a major championship), longevity (long and rich history) or high on controversy. The latter most often stems from much-publicised violence between warring supporter groups.' The Edinburgh Derby comfortably meets two of those three criteria, and the third on occasion. In *The Guardian* newspaper, football journalist Nick Millar wrote that: 'Local rivalries are not quite as simple as mere proximity ... [Nottingham] Forest and Notts County are separated by a river, the clubs' two grounds a few hundred metres apart, but there's little animosity between them.'

'For real animosity to fester,' he goes on, you need 'deep historical differences, feuds, fights, common players and managers, genuine competitiveness. All these things feed great rivalries.'

The Edinburgh Derby has all of these ingredients and more, yet simply put, it exists, as does all Scottish football, in the shadow of the Old Firm, the two biggest, richest, most powerful, loudest and easiest to offend clubs. They dominate to such an extent that the TV coverage of Scottish football is almost constantly Celtic or Rangers versus somebody else. There is barely even a pretence that anyone else matters, except in relation to the Old Firm narrative. And there are other, less obvious reasons why the Edinburgh Derby is not as well known.

Edinburgh is a very famous and successful city in so many other spheres, that shouting about football is not something it has ever really needed to do and, as we shall see, is not something that Edinburgh was ever really likely to do, given the nature of the city and her people. And so, this chance question, asked during small talk between colleagues on the fringe of a small conference, helped to plant the seed of this book.

* * *

One of the first things I learned is that the Edinburgh Derby is the world's oldest derby match. I have lived in Edinburgh for decades, and yet I did not know that. Nobody seems to know it. And with that long history comes all – or most – of the ingredients of a *proper rivalry*. There is too much history, too much fascinating social, religious and ethnic context, at times hatred, at times downright bizarreness, and frankly too much great football and too many great players for this fixture and this rivalry to remain as the forgotten derby. And then there is the history; so much history.

If Heart of Midlothian v Hibernian existed in another city perhaps it would be different. But Edinburgh is a historical, an architectural, a cultural masterpiece in its own right. It attracts attention for many reasons; foreign tourists pack its streets ever year to come and attend the world's largest annual arts festival, thousands of young students move here to attend one of its four universities (including one that is consistently ranked among the top universities in the world), and millions of people travel in and out every year to participate in its economy. Edinburgh is so successful at attracting people to live here that around half of the population are not born in the city. Edinburgh is a melting pot of immigrants; from elsewhere in Scotland, from England, from around the world. Football, because of the unique place it occupies in societies, is a great way to get underneath the skin of a city. To understand its subcultures, its politics, even its nasty side. In Edinburgh, it is where you can go and hear the authentic Edinburgh accent, mixed in with local Scots dialect. In a city known for its success, its beauty and its affluence, it's where you can find the traditional working classes, and a predominantly native Edinburgher crowd.

Nothing matters more to a football fan than their own city rivalry. It might not be the biggest, the most high-stakes, the most high-profile, the most monied, the most watched or of the most interest to Far East TV audiences; but that doesn't matter if it is local to you. It is something that the person with a fleeting interest will never be able to understand fully, because how could they? It is one of the places where football, with all of its modern paraphernalia, all of the media hype, and all of the new-found respectability brought about by slick PR and marketing, still reveals itself in its most raw, uncensored form. It is where fans and players take things too far, it is where atmospheres crackle, and it is where the very soul of a football club is laid bare. It causes grown men to act like toddlers, and provokes emotions that are so intense that it must be impossible for someone alien to football to understand; it must just look ridiculous. It is, in fact, ridiculous.

To people born and raised in Edinburgh, that is what the Edinburgh Derby means. It is the biggest match of almost every season, surpassed only by occasional decisive cup matches. And while the two main Edinburgh clubs have often been run badly, lurched from crisis to crisis, or just limped along in apathetic mediocrity, the rivalry has continued to boil away in the corner, waiting to bubble up every few months, and boil over every once in a while. Edinburghers don't always have a lot to be grateful to the football gods for, but living in such an authentic rivalry is definitely one.

Because while, as we will see, both the Heart of Midlothian Football Club (informally known as Hearts) and the Hibernian Football Club (informally known as Hibs) have generally underachieved, they collectively form the oldest and one of the most historic football rivalries anywhere in world football. For 150 years, these two clubs have had an unbroken rivalry that has stretched to more than 600 matches. And while neither club is among the great names of European football, the rivalry is increasingly unique, and should be cherished as such. In a world of globalisation, or dubious ownership where the wealthy clubs increasingly play at a different level, proper, authentic football is becoming harder to find, and genuine intra-city rivalries are not as common as one might think. In Scotland we have the Old Firm in Glasgow, and there is also the Dundee Derby between Dundee FC and Dundee United FC, two clubs that share not only a city but, in what must be a quite unique arrangement in world football, share the same street (their home grounds, Dens Park and Tannadice respectively, are about 100 metres apart). As far as big, traditional intra-city derbies go, that is it in Scotland. Even in England, there are not many traditional two-club city rivalries: Birmingham, Liverpool, Nottingham, Sheffield, Bristol, Stoke-on-Trent and Manchester.

This book will spend some time examining the nature, character and history of Edinburgh. This is not done simply to indulge myself, even though Edinburgh is a subject that I never tire of researching and writing about. It is in fact to show how the city impacts upon her football clubs, how her nature and history and geography helped to shape the rivalry. It will hopefully become clear that Edinburgh is a city that does not need her football clubs, she does not rely on them for fame, or amusement, or profile, or revenue. Edinburgh will never be best known for its football clubs in the way that Glasgow is for the Old Firm, or Newcastle is for Newcastle United. That says as much about the success and vibrancy of the city as it does about the relative obscurity of the clubs, although at times the clubs have made it easy for outsiders to disregard them. As a capital city and a centre of literature, learning, science, finance, religion, history, culture and festivals, tourism, politics and of other sports – particularly rugby and golf – both Hearts and Hibernian would have to up their level of achievement to something approaching that of FC Barcelona to become Edinburgh's best-known attraction. But the fact that they come from such a storied and historic city does not diminish them, their achievements and their rivalry. Indeed, I would argue it makes the story more interesting, more compelling, bestowing upon it a character and history that is unique.

It is also an important facet in understanding the indifference with which elements of Edinburgh society have treated their football clubs. Leaving aside for a moment the obvious social class distinction, the fact that corporate Edinburgh, for want of a better name, has largely ignored its two clubs (although this has started to change recently) and has instead ploughed its backing and sponsorship into rugby and the various festivals in Edinburgh is interesting. Edinburgh is a city used to success, and why would you waste your sponsorship millions on the mediocre football clubs when you could instead associate your company name with the world's largest arts festival, or one of the most iconic and successful annual sports tournaments in world sport, the rugby Six Nations Championship, with its international exposure and huge TV audiences?

In fact, a good argument could be made that rivalry matters more when it is between two clubs who probably will not win trophies; the significance of 'winning' the derby matches becomes an even higher priority, in the absence of cups, European runs or league trophies to strive for. And so while the size of the club and number of fans has to be included as a factor in the nature of a rivalry, it cannot be *the* factor, otherwise we are giving up yet another aspect of our game to be owned and competed for solely by the big, rich clubs.

The Edinburgh Derby will never be one of the world's biggest, but biggest is not always best. Having been lucky enough to attend El Clásico at the Nou Camp, I can honestly say that the atmosphere was a disappointment, lacking in the aggression and anger that fuels the atmospheres of many great derbies. This is no doubt in part due to the almost complete absence of opposing supporters, but it seemed almost to be a deeper factor, something intrinsic in the fans that is different to the fans at derbies in the UK that I have experienced first-hand. The Edinburgh Derby may not be a patch on Barça v Real Madrid in almost any measure you care to think of, but I can testify that the atmosphere at some Edinburgh Derbies has been better than it was in the Nou Camp that evening – more intense, more aggressive, more explosive, more singing (something that Spanish fans seemed far less inclined to partake in than their Scottish or UK counterparts) and more laced with that X factor that makes an atmosphere what it is: an imprecise combination of anticipation, jeopardy, nerves, intimidation, excitement and, often, hatred.

I write this not as some cack-handed attempt at one-upmanship, but rather to demonstrate that big clubs, with lots of money and lots of fans, absolutely do not have a monopoly on rivalry, on passion and feeling for their club.

Neither Hibernian nor Hearts will ever be the aristocracy of European football: they have enough trouble trying to bother the aristocracy of Scottish football. But that does not mean that they do not have an intense, history-laden rivalry that is rich in baggage and subplots.

There may be positive aspects to rivalries but it would be a stretch to claim that they are a universally positive aspect of football. Few are known for their friendliness, and the most famous are generally those with the most needle, and so if we accept that the vast majority of rivalries are defined by 'needle', then it follows that the nature of any specific rivalry can be truly found in identifying what exactly are the causes of the needle, and indeed there is a whole academic discipline dedicated to the detail and the causes. The aim of this book isn't to go into depth about great matches or the minutiae of individual seasons, but instead to look at the causes of the rivalry; why did it come about that these two clubs became such bitter rivals, and what has sustained it over 150 years?

One problem with looking at it is how to deal with the facts and figures, and as always when dealing with statistics, there are different ways these can be cut. When looking at head-to-heads, I have included all of the local competitions up to the point they stopped being relevant. While these can often be written off as 'non-competitive', that is to reduce the significance with which they were viewed at the time; the local competitions mattered hugely, and while they did start to fall away as the national competitions gained in significance, and the League Cup established itself post-war, the East of Scotland Shield remained a significant occasion into the late 70s/early 80s, something that football historian Andy Mitchell confirmed when interviewed for this book. In the early years, the local competitions were effectively what today you would think of as domestic competitions, the bread and butter of a club. The Scottish Cup was more akin to the European Cup. It is also worth remembering that unlike today, the clubs did not face each other four times a season in the league. Looking through the history books, it is amazing how uniform the derby scheduling was in the league season, with the first league match being played around September, the second on New Year's Day.

When reading this, there will be views and opinions, perhaps whole sections or chapters, that partisan supporters of each club will not like. Football fans see only the good in their team's actions, and only conspiracy, plot and evil on those of the other. And where their club has been caught out, even when bang to rights, they defend, they mitigate, they point to others who are worse. That is how football fans are; your club is uniquely virtuous among all others in the world of football. But of course that is nonsense, and it would be strange that, if over the course of 150 years, both clubs had not at various times been both sinned against and sinner. Most of life exists in a shade of grey, not in black and white, and that is certainly true of 150 years of footballing rivalry.

And in football, truth is a rare commodity. Instead, we have competing narratives, myths and truths, and who can say which is right? In every incident, the aggressor will be fuelled by the righteous indignation of some past precedent, slight, or transgression. In Edinburgh, each side will have its own interpretation of events, and they are often quite different. Some would have been true, some have been distorted by time and inconvenience, and I daresay many have been deliberately lost to the official histories which are responsible for much of myth-building around their clubs. In this book, I will try to present the absolute truths (scores, results, established facts – although even these are not without their challenges), but also the different perspectives. I will present these not because I believe them but because the people who have contributed to this work believe them, and at least some of the supporters believe them. This book will largely exist in shades of grey, as does much of the rivalry I seek to explore and understand.

But this will require a degree of indulgence from the readers, particularly those who are followers of one or other of the teams. There will be things in here that you do not like, and some things that you might not agree with. That's as it should be, and all history, let alone football rivalry history, is contested and disputed. I do not intend this to be a puff piece to make one set of fans feel good or bad; there are umpteen club histories that will give you the rose-tinted view of your club's history from that perspective. And where there are particularly contentious issues, I will do my best to present them as fairly as possible. I won't succeed in this, and I am certain that at various points fans of either club will not like what they read. But I do give the undertaking that this is written in good faith, and with the aim of marking 150 years of one of world football's great rivalries.

CHAPTER 2

EDINBURGH

WALKING ALONG the Cowgate today, I am still struck by how narrow and enclosed it is. Tall tenement buildings on either side create a long gorge of a street, which is spanned by the two bridges that cross over the top. There are old churches and chapels, and flats where actual people from Edinburgh still live all looming up on either side of the road. For its entire length, cobbled streets and dark, damp closes run off at right angles, rising steeply on either side. Where there are modern buildings, they are built in a style that is sympathetic to their surroundings – tightly packed, overbearing even. It is an odd part of the city, in effect a single long street, but such is its location it has a cut-off feel despite being in the heart of Edinburgh's historic Old Town. It is not difficult to see how a disliked minority could be left down here and ignored by the respectable city going about its business in the streets above; it's not hard to see how it could become a ghetto.

There are still a few signs of this area's former life as Edinburgh's 'Little Ireland' enclave. There are unofficial Little Ireland street signs that have been put up next to the official street names. There is a plaque in remembrance of one of Little Ireland's famous sons, the great Irish nationalist leader James Connolly. There are old schools and pubs, and at its eastern end, where the streetscape broadens out slightly, there are gardens that host a smart, almost classical building that is set back from the street: St Patrick's Church, the centre of the old Irish Catholic community that lived there. St Patrick's Church is the proud home of an early football trophy that was once played for by all of Edinburgh in those early years of Association football – the Edinburgh Football Association Cup. This trophy was last played for in 1881 after Hibernian Football Club defeated St Bernard's to win the cup for the third straight year; Hibernian had won the trophy outright, and the competition was renamed the Edinburgh Shield (and later the East of Scotland Shield). For ever more, the Edinburgh FA Cup, the most prestigious trophy in Edinburgh football and a de facto domestic championship in those early years, would remain in the possession of St Patrick's Church, Hibernian FC's spiritual home in the small district and community from which they had sprung in the Cowgate (or 'Coogate', as it was known by those who lived there).

* * *

Many books on Edinburgh begin with geology, which might seem like a strange place to start I agree, but you don't have to spend much time in Scotland's capital city to understand why. And as the setting of the Cowgate testifies, Edinburgh's geology has dominated its history: its seven hills, the rises and falls of its land, the deep valleys, such as the one the Cowgate sits in. The scientific discipline itself was pioneered here by James Hutton, the 'Father of Geology'. In fact, one of Edinburgh's many museums, Dynamic Earth, is dedicated to the history of our planet and is situated, in a brilliant and ironic example of the regeneration of the Old Town, in one of the former breweries right beneath the imposing Salisbury Crags.[1] Incidentally, and even more appropriately, the new Scottish Parliament which was completed in 2004 sits right next door on the site of the same former brewery. 'Edinburgh's chief assets are her natural beauties,' wrote Edinburgh writer Rosaline Masson of both Arthur's Seat and Salisbury Crags; 'Where is there another city with great mountains and great cliffs rising from its midst?' Writer and poet Edwin Muir observed that the 'first obvious impression that Edinburgh produces is of a rocky splendour and pride. It is a city built upon rock and guarded by rock. The old town is perched on the ridge which runs up from Holyrood to the Castle, and on the other side, to the east, rise the two shapes of the Salisbury Crag and Arthur's Seat.' And writing in the mid-19th century, Scottish geologist Hugh Miller wrote that 'the Scottish capital is one of the few cities of the [British] empire that possess natural features, and which, were the buildings away, would, while it ceased to be a town, become a very picturesque country. And hence one of the peculiar characteristics of Edinburgh. The natural features so overtop the artificial ones – its hollow valleys as so much more strongly marked than its streets, and its hills and precipices than its buildings ... the intelligent visitors ... are led to conceive of it rather as a great country place than as a great town. It is a scene of harmonious contrasts.'

And if geology seems a bit removed from the story of a great football rivalry, allow me to point out Heart of Midlothian's official club song, 'Hearts, Hearts, Glorious Hearts':

> Our forwards can score and it's no idle talk,
> Our defence is as strong as the old Castle Rock.

The 'old Castle Rock' being the mount of black volcanic rock that Edinburgh Castle sits atop, and which has repelled invading armies for centuries; as a comparison for a team's defence, it is as good as it's possible to get.

The geology of the city is so important because it has helped to define Edinburgh physically, but also socially and culturally. The Castle Rock is the historic birthplace of the city. A notable defensive feature, it has been settled since at least Roman times by the ancient British Celts who inhabited the area, the *Votadini*. By the 6th century AD the names *Eidyn* and *Din Eidyn* – meaning 'Fort Eidyn' – were recorded for the first time. Anglicans and Gaels interpreted the name after their own languages, giving us *Edineburg* and *Dunedene* respectively; thus, in English she is called *Edinburgh* and in Scots Gaelic, *Dunedin*.[2]

Sloping down from the top of the Castle Rock to the east is a long ridge, known in geology as a 'crag and tail', and as those early Celts spread out from their defensive site on Castle Rock, they could only go in one direction, and that was eastwards down the mile-long tail. Hence Edinburgh grew down along this narrow ridge, which became the Royal Mile. The famous narrow, winding streets, known as closes or wynds, spread out at right angles from the Royal Mile and down the steep flanks of the ridge. The Old Town of Edinburgh is literally shaped by the lie of the land, and when looking at old street maps it looks remarkably like the skeleton of a fish, with a single, long backbone and hundreds of smaller bones branching off at right angles (the Cowgate sits at the bottom of this ridge on the southern side; Princes Street Gardens and the New Town sit on the northern side).

For as long as Scotland and England remained at war, this was how Edinburgh stayed. The downside of being the capital and centre of so much of Scottish life was that it was always a target for invading English armies, and so staying within the city walls was necessary. Thus, it became a cramped and overcrowded warren, and is credited with being one of the first high-rise cities anywhere in the world, as the only direction in which the city could grow was upwards, often to nine or ten storeys and some buildings were even as high as 14 storeys, skyscraper territory by medieval standards. It is why the city is to this day dominated by tall tenement buildings, and the sense of a lack of space, while no longer as pronounced as once was, can still be easily felt in the Old Town, even if many of the closes were eventually widened into streets to allow horses and carts and later cars to use them.

Eventually the threat of English invasion receded, firstly when the Scottish and English crowns were united under the Scottish King James VI and secondly, and more formally, when the two countries were united by the Act of Union in 1707, which created the present-day United Kingdom. With the peace secured, Edinburgh could break out of its defensive position, and expand beyond its walls, although the city was shorn of its status as a European capital city by the Union. This freedom to expand had a profound effect on Edinburgh and on the shape and development of both its town and people. For centuries, the nobility had lived cheek-by-jowl with the lowest peasants: 'These houses, with their dark, stone staircases housed several families, causing many people to refer to them as "vertical streets", and it is true that all social levels could be found on one stair … Edinburgh, with a population of 57,000 crowded into its spine of rock, was more democratic than many eighteenth-century cities.'[3] Respectable Edinburgh may have tolerated such proximity and overcrowding when the threat of invasion loomed, but they quickly used the peace to plan the physical separation of the city. A contemporary report on 'proposals for carrying on certain public works in the city' laid out the natural advantages of the location of Edinburgh, being in such a setting and having the Firth (estuary) of Forth just to the north, but then went on to list the disadvantages 'without number' that outweigh them:

Placed upon the ridge of a hill, it admits of but one good street, running from east to west [The Royal Mile]; and even this is tolerably accessible only from one quarter. The narrow lanes leading to the north and south, by reason of their steepness, narrowness, and dirtiness, can only be considered as so many unavoidable nuisances ... the houses stand more crowded than in any other town in Europe, and are built to a height that is almost incredible. Hence necessarily follows a great want of free air, light, cleanliness, and every other comfortable accommodation. Hence also families, sometimes no less than ten or a dozen, are obliged to live overhead of each other in the same building.[4]

It was at this point that the New Town was planned and built, on empty land just to the north of the Old Town, across one of the valleys. The bottom of the valley, which was for centuries a cesspool of Edinburgh's filth, was drained, and is now where Edinburgh's main train station, Waverley Station,[5] sits in between the Old and New Towns. The creation of the New Town saw the Old Town deserted by most of those who had the means, and created an unmistakeable separation of the classes; the Old Town became a forgotten, avoided slum for the poor and unfortunates – including the Irish immigrants – while the New Town became a concentration of wealth and sophistication. Edinburgh's character had always had a schizophrenic element to it, but now those different traits were unmistakably laid out for all to see. One side an elegant, symmetrical streetscape of wide boulevards and neoclassical design, the physical embodiment of 18th-century rationality and order; the other side a jumbled mess of haphazard passageways and buildings, none of it really making sense, beset by poverty and squalor. To cross the North Bridge (an extension of the aforementioned South Bridge that spans the Cowgate), which was constructed to connect the two separate parts of Edinburgh, was to cross from one era to another.

* * *

My grandfather would take me on walks around Leith when I was a wee boy. It was where he was born and raised and he loved walking me around it. He was a policeman in Leith after the war, and he would show me the docks, his old police boxes, the tenement in which he was born, the old shop where his mother sold sweets, and Leith Hospital, where my grandmother worked when they first met at a dance for young policemen and young nurses. I well remember the bustle in the streets, some of the characters you would see walking around and, even to my young eyes, some of the obvious poverty; Leith in the mid-1980s had not been regenerated, it had not become trendy and like many post-industrial areas, it felt down on its luck. It felt far away from Edinburgh and different. Great Junction Street and the *fit o' the walk* (foot of the walk) were equivalents to the High Street in any large town in Scotland.

Leith is a port town, and for most of its history it was a separate and significant place in its own right. For centuries it was Scotland's main port, before maritime interests moved to the west coast with the rise of transatlantic trade. It had its own council, its own tram system (that was incompatible with Edinburgh's, meaning passengers would have to get off one set of trams and board another to continue their journey), its own town hall and its own train station. It was, in every sense, a town, and to people of my grandfather's generation, it stayed that way, despite it being merged with Edinburgh in 1920. At the time of the merger, an unofficial referendum saw Leithers reject the proposed merger with 26,810 votes against, and just 4,340 in favour.

Today, Leith is quite an extreme mix, a place where a Michelin-starred restaurant can be found on the same street as an enormous block of brutalist 1960s-style high-rise flats that became notorious as a home to prostitution and drug abuse. Leith still plays host to some towering blocks of flats (some of the few left in Edinburgh), and some areas of obvious social deprivation. And at the same time, there are numerous new developments of flats with trendy penthouses, converted warehouses, and the accompanying amenities of hairdressers, restaurants and bars. It is a stark example of the clash between regeneration and gentrification; at what point does 'regenerating' an area change it beyond recognition and force out the long-time residents? It is a question that many cities face. Leith is undoubtedly a 'nicer' place to visit now than it was in the

1980s. But if you are a born-and-bred Leither, who valued bumping into people you knew and shopping and drinking in traditional shops and bars, the price of having young professionals flood the area might not be worth it.

Despite the regeneration, Leith does still have the feel of a separate town within a city. Its main streets are busy and bustling, and it is the most densely populated area of Scotland. In large part that is because Leith is a town of traditional tenements where there are very few low-rise houses, and so people live closely packed in, close to their neighbours. Perhaps this density contributes to the sense of community? It undoubtedly gives the place a sense of bustle and vibrancy.

Back around the time that the Little Ireland community was forming in the Cowgate, so Leith was developing its own Irish community, again drawn to the town by its industry. This community centred around the St Mary Star of the Sea/ Stella Maris Catholic Church, a community that would do much to help save and then grow Hibernian FC in its early years, as Leith became Hibernian's adopted home. Today, the area is closely associated with the club, and Hibernian's (unofficial) club anthem is 'Sunshine on Leith', a song by the Scottish folk duo The Proclaimers, who are Hibernian supporters. Easter Road almost straddles the border between Leith and Edinburgh (the Easter refers not to the holiday, but to its place at the eastern end of Leith), which could just as easily be a metaphor for the club over the decades.

It is one of the joys of football in Edinburgh that both clubs remain firmly rooted in their home communities, and Gorgie without Hearts or Leith without Hibernian would be poorer places for their absence. But both clubs also claim to represent the whole city, to be the 'pride of Edinburgh', or specifically, in Hearts' case, the 'heart and soul of Edinburgh'. In reality you will find Hibernian and Hearts fans scattered across the city, and indeed further afield. This is often due to the way in which the traditional areas of the city were cleared and redeveloped, with people from those districts moved out of inner-city areas and relocated to new housing estates on the edge of town. To this day 'the parliamentary constituencies that account for the majority of Hearts support are Edinburgh West, Edinburgh South West and Edinburgh South. Hibs draw a considerable amount of their support from two other Edinburgh constituencies – Edinburgh North and Leith and Edinburgh East.'[6]

* * *

Where I went to primary school in Edinburgh was not far from the Gorgie district and its surrounding areas of Dalry, Fountainbridge and North Merchiston. In fact, my primary school was regularly within smelling distance. I don't mean that in an unkind way; anyone who was brought up in Edinburgh will instantly know the *very* distinctive smell that the breweries and distilleries give off, the smell of roasting malt and barley, that on certain days would drift over my school. It's not a bad smell, but it's quite hard to describe. When speaking to Hearts fans, it has been described to me variously as bread toasting, or bacon being cooked. There is still the odd brewery and distillery in the area but on nothing like the scale there used to be, and that smell isn't as strong as it once was, but it's still there.

Edinburgh became a brewing centre, partly due to its ready supply of fresh water and, at its peak, produced one third of all the beer consumed in the entire British Empire. As the city expanded, entire districts sprang up to serve this industry, and the area most associated with brewing runs south-west from the city centre. This wedge of industrial Edinburgh followed the line of the Union Canal and the railways, creating a long, linear community: Fountainbridge, Dalry and Gorgie. They became and remain closely associated with Heart of Midlothian. Gorgie is one of the city's old industrial districts, and it still has an industrial look and feel to it, even if the breweries are mostly gone; the tenements are tightly packed and built in a utilitarian style to house the thousands of workers in the area. Hearts' stadium, Tynecastle Park, sits almost on the main road, and is the beating heart (no pun intended) of this district. It is a fitting location for a football stadium, at the centre of its community in the middle of dense housing and industrial warehouses; very L.S. Lowry. There is barely an old photo of a match at Tynecastle without either huge warehouses with triangular roofs, or tall tenements towering over the crowd.

And while Gorgie/Dalry and its brewing industry quickly became associated with Hearts, it has another side-effect which would be essential for the creation of the contemporary football landscape. The breweries and their associated industries needed transport, and in those days that meant canals. And so in 1822 the Union Canal was dug between Fountainbridge in Edinburgh all the way to Glasgow and its access to export markets via the Atlantic. The construction of the canal relied on immigrant Irish labour (Ireland was then part of Britain) and with it the emergence of a distinctly Irish immigrant community in Edinburgh, from where Hibernian Football Club would grow, down in the Cowgate. That community were – due to the geography of Edinburgh – literally the underclass. But as 'respectable' Edinburgh went about its business on the bridges above, this community was coalescing around St Patrick's Church and Father (later Canon) Hannan, whose idea was to create a healthy activity for the young men of his parish. Little did he know that he was helping to create the world's oldest football derby.

CHAPTER 3

THE NEEDLE MATCH

1874–1887

A HORSE-DRAWN cab speeds its way up the long, narrow road into town. In the cab is a very nervous man, and well he might be, for chasing him is a baying mob. The man manages to hold them off using the cab driver's whip, and make his escape into a nearby friend's house. Angry at losing him, the mob set about destroying the taxi instead.

It was spring 1878. Queen Victoria sat on the throne, Benjamin Disraeli was the Prime Minister, the UK was preparing to go to war with Russia and had moved its mighty naval fleet to the Dardanelles in preparation; the world's longest bridge, spanning the Forth of Tay, was about to be completed. And the man being chased was Tom Purdie, captain and early driving force behind the Heart of Midlothian Football Club, who had just beaten Hibernian Football Club 3-2 in the final of the Edinburgh Association Cup, the most important trophy in early Edinburgh football.

I say 'final'; it was in fact a series of finals that had become more like a Test series in cricket. After the first match was drawn, four further replays were required to decide the fate of the trophy; for both sides, it was their first cup final, and would be their first trophy. Across this five-match marathon there was controversy aplenty: rough play; disallowed goals; bumper attendances (and gate receipts); crowd trouble; goals that never crossed the line (allegedly); over-the-top celebrations (allegedly); a raising of the prices to dissuade the 'less desirable' elements from attending; disagreements about the agreed rules and (alleged) displays of bad faith; yet more crowd trouble including the storming of the entrance gate (due to those high prices?); controversial decisions by the Association; a refused handshake (allegedly); and yet more crowd trouble, which culminated in the Hearts captain being chased up the road. The angry men pursuing Purdie were described as a 'mob of roughs' angry at the result, or as fanatical supporters avenging a lack of sportsmanship and grace; they followed the Hibernian Football Club. It is not difficult to see why these two teams would quickly become the greatest of rivals.

Early football history can be scratchy and unreliable. Records, where they were accurately kept, have often been lost. Living memory has long since faded, very often the places in which these events took place are no longer with us, swept away as our towns and cities have expanded. This difficulty is compounded when looking at a football rivalry, where the exact same events and 'facts' can and will be perceived and presented differently. This is not to say either of them is wrong per se, but it is only natural that club historians, both amateur and official, will have over the years emphasised the positives and minimised the negatives (if they even included the negatives at all). But such is the nature of rivalry, and for this we cannot simply blame history. Even in these times of TV replays, two fans wearing different-coloured scarves will often see the exact same, high-definition, super-slow-motion action replay very differently. Football is a highly subjective and overly emotive game, and undisputed, untainted facts are rare. This cup final is a case in point.

The first match was played at Mayfield Park, which was then just to the south of the city. To walk around the Mayfield area of Edinburgh today is a pleasurable experience; a mostly middle-class residential area, that has a large university campus, and sits not far from the bottom of one of Edinburgh's seven hills, Blackford Hill. It is where one of the old main roads south from Edinburgh – Causewayside – runs, making access straightforward. So it is not surprising that Mayfield played host to some of Edinburgh's earliest matches. Both the Mayfield and Powburn (a neighbouring ground) were central to the story of early football in Edinburgh. And so it was here in this suburb that the rivalry between two of the city's football clubs really started to bite, a rivalry that would become the oldest city derby in the world. Inevitably, the cause and the blame for the dispute that ignited the rivalry is disputed; how could it be any other way?

The original final of the Edinburgh FA Cup took place on Saturday, 9 February 1878. Contemporary reports tell us that 'the Heart(s) did not seem to be altogether in trim, but the Hibernians played exceedingly well'.

The match was drawn and Hibernian were reportedly unhappy at the end of the match, having had two goals disallowed without explanation, but were confident of winning the replay as they were the fitter team, and the Edinburgh FA had decreed that in the event of another draw, 30 minutes of extra time would be played.

Or had they?

The second match caught the public imagination and a large crowd of more than 1,000 turned up to see a more exciting game, despite terrible weather. Hearts took the lead after half an hour when a free kick was put into the box, and 'out of the scrimmage which ensued the ball was headed through the Irish goal-posts amid great cheering'. The game then seems to have become an end-to-end battle, with the Hibernian team having the better of it. With just five minutes left, the pressure told. Hibernian player Donnelly had run the ball 'prettily' down the right and his cross was shot through the goal. This apparently sparked 'a scene of the wildest enthusiasm, the Irishmen tossing their hats and jumping and cheering for several minutes while the players were mobbed by their enthusiastic partisans'. The match finished 1-1, and with their superior fitness and the momentum from the late equaliser, Hibernian were ready for extra time, but Hearts captain Tom Purdie had other ideas. Purdie refused to play the additional 30 minutes as he was not happy with the Hibernian equaliser and intended to protest to the Edinburgh FA about it. The reports do not specify whether it was the goal itself, or the wild celebrations and pitch invasion of the Hibernian supporters that he was unhappy about; possibly it was both. The suspicion in the Hibernian camp was that he did not think his exhausted team were up to an additional 30 minutes.

In Purdie's defence, it is reported that, as he understood it, it was in the gift of the two captains to decide whether to play the extra time and given his grievance with the manner of Hibernian's goal, he was not going to agree. The Hibernian appeals to play on are described by Albert Mackie, a pre-war football journalist and Hearts historian, as 'demonstrative', indicating a genuine sense of grievance on their part. It was also conceded that perhaps Purdie's attitude to this helped to 'get the Irishmen's goat' and contributed to their attack on him after the fifth and final match in the series. But the anger didn't have to wait until then, as Purdie's refusal sparked several fights amongst the rival fans who, as we have seen from the earlier descriptions, were already in combustible mood.

It is impossible to judge the validity or otherwise of both side's claims, and while Hibernian do seem to have been genuinely angry, the same could be said for Purdie and Hearts, who took their grievance to the Edinburgh FA. The Association then managed to rile both sides with their judgement. Hearts' complaint was dismissed as a 'complete waste of time', which to Hibernian ears meant they were robbed of their opportunity to press home an advantage and should have been awarded the cup as Hearts had forfeited. But the Association stayed silent on Hearts' refusal to play the extra time, which does suggest there was at least some ambiguity in the rules. With both teams nursing a sense of injustice, and a few of the supporters nursing black eyes, the final went to a third match in the space of two weeks.

The third match again attracted well over 1,000 spectators, despite the fact that the Edinburgh FA had raised the prices in a bid to keep the crowd 'select', after the fighting that had taken place last time. Hibernian this time scored first, and their sense of grievance rose again when another goal to put them two-up was disallowed, again without explanation – the third Hibernian goal in the three matches so far to be disallowed. Along with the Edinburgh FA's apparent ignoring of the fact that Hearts had refused to play the extra time in the previous replay, it is a safe assumption that the Hibernian players and supporters may have been feeling that familiar sense of injustice at the hands of the authorities. That sense of anger again manifested itself physically after Hearts equalised the match. On hearing the goal had been scored, a 900-strong mob of Hibernian supporters who had not been admitted (obviously these Irish navvies were not 'select' enough to pay for entry) stormed the gate, and pushed their way through into the ground. Despite this, no more trouble was reported, and the match again ended in stalemate.

The third replay (the fourth match overall) was moved to a new venue in the Merchiston district of the city, an area that was more urban, and is not far from Gorgie, that would go on to become so closely associated with Hearts. It was by now April, and another strong crowd of 1,500 turned up – apparently swelled by a number of rugby players who had come along to watch the other code's 'needle match'. The infamy of this struggle was gaining wider recognition, and generating money for the Association already. This game was reported as rough and keenly fought, but there was no further crowd trouble, and the game again ended in a 1-1 draw, Hearts taking the lead before Hibernian equalised. Again, extra time had been mandated, and it was played without reported arguments and no further goals. A report from *The Scotsman* newspaper described the action:

> Play in previous matches had been noted for its roughness, but that on the present occasion excelled in that respect – heavy and unnecessary charging, rash back kicking and an almost total want of dribbling and passing completely spoiling the beauties of the Association game. If the committee of the Association wish the game to take root in the East of Scotland, they will require to follow the example of the West, and discourage a repetition of such a display of charging as that witnessed on Saturday.

It sounds very much like a derby match, and it is funny that the above passage – or certainly the sentiments contained within, if not the exact Victorian language – could be used to describe a high number of Edinburgh Derbies throughout its 150 years. It also again highlights just how local football was in these early days, that the game in the west could be noted for its different characteristics as if it were taking place in another country entirely.

The fourth replay, and fifth and final match overall, was moved back to Mayfield, this time to Powburn, which was the home of the first of the Edinburgh association clubs, 3rd Edinburgh Rifle Volunteers. Another bumper crowd was attracted, and this time they saw an absorbing match. At half-time it was 0-0, despite several near misses for Hibernian which had apparently dispirited their players and support. Hibernian did manage to take the lead early in the second half, when Hearts goalkeeper Jake Reid's clearance was intercepted by Hibernian captain Michael Whelahan, who shot it straight back and into the goal. Hearts equalised through J. Alexander, before Hibernian again took the lead after another mistake from goalkeeper Reid, who fumbled a shot from Owen Quinn into the goal. George Mitchell levelled for Hearts, and they went on to grab the winner, through J. Alexander again. 'And then in a hotly disputed goalmouth scramble the referee awarded Hearts a third goal, although many thought the ball had not crossed the line.'[7]

Regardless of the Hibernian indignation, the goal was awarded amidst the crowd cheering, and after the marathon five-match final, Hearts had won the Edinburgh Cup. Mackie described the aftermath:

> [Hearts captain] Purdie had played a great and
> clever game, but he left the field followed by a

mob of roughs (none of them Hibernian players) who were annoyed at the result and who chased him from Powburn Toll to Causewayside. It was on this occasion that the Hearts captain laid about them with the cabby's whip.

The Hibernian version of events, as put forward by Hibernian's historian Alan Lugton, differs:

> At the end of the match Michael Whelahan extended the hand of friendship to Tom Purdie, who roughly pushed him aside. There was no trouble with the players, but the navvies [the Hibernian support were often referred to as 'navvies' or 'Irish navvies', a nickname for Irish manual labourers] had seen this slight on their captain and when Tom Purdie left the ground in his carriage, they gave chase … to Causewayside, where the Hearts player abandoned his carriage and took refuge in a friend's house. Unable to find him, the navvies turned on his carriage and wrecked it.

The event was serious enough that Father Hannan (effectively the Hibernian chairman at the time) had to appeal from his pulpit (for the second time during the series of finals) for better behaviour, telling his parishioners that such behaviour 'brought ill-fame on Hibernian and the Irish Catholic community who did not in any way countenance violence or unchristian acts'.

Whether or not these 'violent and unchristian acts' were provoked will never be known. But we can say with certainty that this series of finals really ignited the rivalry; five high-stakes matches almost back-to-back with all of the inevitable niggles, perceived injustices, rough play, crowd trouble and annoyances that emerged were the kindling that was required for the spark of football to really catch in Edinburgh. However, the initial antipathy between the clubs seems to have come earlier, when they met in the Scottish Cup for the first time in September 1877.

Describing the tie, Lugton states that Hibernian were 'drawn against Hearts who were quickly becoming their keenest rivals'. It is examined in more depth elsewhere but it does bear repeating that Hibernian had no shortage of potential rivals. A club with their background who were so unapologetically and, as it turned out on numerous occasions, muscularly (both on and off the field) representing and defending such a hated community were never going to be warmly accepted. One contemporary journalist wrote on the creation of an Irish Catholic club: 'This must have been a tremendous undertaking at such a time; for the Irish in Scotland, and more especially in the city of John Knox, were by far the least popular section of the community, to put it mildly.'[8]

Ironically, though, this isolation helped Hibernian quickly establish themselves as the dominant club in the city, as they had a captive market of players from which to choose, not to mention a large and boisterous support. None of the other emerging Edinburgh clubs could, nor would they want to, compete with Hibernian for the affections of the Irish immigrant community. This straightaway placed Hibernian towards the top of the newly emerging Edinburgh game and made them a very obvious target to be shot at. And it quickly became Hearts who would do the shooting.

The historical record is light on why it was Hearts that emerged from the many clubs to become the champion. When I asked Andy Mitchell why he thinks it was Hearts, and not say St Bernard's or Hanover (who, as he points out, both have thematic, slightly theatrical names rooted in Edinburgh, as do Hearts), he talked about their infrastructure. Hearts settling in Gorgie relatively early allowed them to move on from the nomadic existence most clubs still had, and so having their own ground set them apart from their rivals at the time. And the localised nature of football, including the early stages of the Scottish Cup which were regionalised, meant they would begin to meet regularly, and often in particularly high-stakes matches, such as that 1878 Edinburgh Cup Final.

Hearts and Hibernian had first played on Christmas Day 1875, when Hearts won 1-0 despite playing three men down for 20 minutes. Hearts actually risked the wrath of the Edinburgh FA in playing Hibs, as the EFA had excluded Hibernian from organised football on the grounds of their nationality and religion. Their next match together was drawn, and then Hibernian got their revenge by winning the following two matches 1-0. The fact that there were over 1,000 spectators at the match shows it had caught the imagination of the public from early on.

In a portent of what was to come in just a few months when the clubs contested their first ever cup final – that mammoth, five-match 1878 Edinburgh Cup tie – their first Scottish Cup match ended in a hard-fought 0-0 draw, but Hibernian emerged to win the replay 2-1. These were only the fifth and sixth times the clubs had met, and there had yet to be more than a single goal to separate them. Lugton states:

> The Hearts fans and players were furious at this Scottish Cup defeat at the hands of the 'inferior Irish' and fighting broke out as the navvies celebrated. Relations between the clubs had never been very good but now things were badly soured and for many years to come Hearts never missed an opportunity to attack Hibernian in the committee rooms of the Edinburgh FA, with a view to having them thrown out of the association.

Another early historian of Hearts who was contemporary to many of the early tussles between the clubs was William Reid, who wrote Hearts' official 50th anniversary history in 1924. He shed a little more light on the growing dislike between the clubs: 'It is on record that on the occasion of one of the first meetings of the clubs in the Scottish Cup competition the Hearts players went to Easter Road stripped for the fray and neither entered the pavilion of their opponents before nor after the match', a snub of such significance that it merited comment in Hearts' official history.

The obvious question is how can a sport in its infancy, and two clubs only three and four years old respectively, have already built up such animosity and provoke such fury in their fans?

'Interest in the game in Edinburgh was really created by the old-time meetings of the Hearts and the Hibernians, into which there then entered racial jealousy, even sectarian bitterness,' wrote Reid in his Hearts history. It is a point with which Andy Mitchell reluctantly agreed.

'I hesitate to go down the religious route,' he tells me, 'but you had a club that represented the Irish Catholic community, who were heavily discriminated against and despised, and so it's understandable that they felt they had a lot to fight against. They were the outsiders to Edinburgh and to Edinburgh football, and on the flip side I think Hearts enthusiastically took on the mantle of being the champions of Edinburgh and her people, of becoming the Edinburgh Club.'

Such animosity does provide some useful context to the Edinburgh Cup Final of 1878, and helps to explain why both the supporters and the players were so combustible. The behaviour of the Hibernian supporters, who had almost instantly gained a reputation for both violence and fanaticism, no doubt played a part, reinforcing some of the worst stereotypes about the Irish. This was obviously not lost on Father Hannan, who had scolded his flock twice during the five-match final for their behaviour and how it reflected upon their community. It must surely have added to the belief that these Irishmen had no business mixing it with respectable Edinburgh.

After the 1878 final the clubs didn't meet again for 11 months, an unusually long time. It is not clear what the reason for this was, but it would not be a surprise if it was at least partly due to the antipathy between the clubs. Regardless of the reason, it turned out that absence certainly had not made Hearts (or indeed Hibs) grow fonder. That the next meeting was to be the final of the very same competition must have added some extra spice to the occasion, which would very much have been seen as a continuation of the needle matches from 1878. As we will see, 11 months was not long enough to allow the grudges to be forgotten, by players or by the supporters. As Mackie wrote: 'The "needle" element, and the fact that Hearts and Hibs were proving themselves the two leading Edinburgh teams, accounted for the 4,000 crowd.'

The final was played, we are told, at a furious pace and both goalkeepers played fine matches. Again, there was to be controversy and crowd trouble. Hibernian took the lead, a goal which 'aroused the Celtic enthusiasm to which spectators at Hearts–Hibs matches were by now accustomed.' There was yet more goal controversy, as Hibernian's opener was apparently influenced by crowd encroachment, which inhibited the Hearts goalkeeper from saving the shot.

It stayed 1-0 until the very last minute when Hearts equalised, despite the Hibernian supporters being sure that time was up. The goal came about from a goalmouth scramble, and the Hibernian players also protested strongly that the goal should have been disallowed due to a foul. The referee disagreed and the goal stood. Another Edinburgh Cup Final between the two was a draw and would go to a replay. And another Edinburgh Cup Final would descend into violence. The Hibernian supporters, furious at the goal being allowed to stand, invaded the pitch and attacked the Hearts players. For their part, the Hearts supporters also invaded in celebration, and hoisted both their goalscorer and their captain shoulder-high to hail the late goal. According to Mackie:

> Although the success of the Hearts in averting a win by their formidable opponents was popular with most of the crowd, the roughs who wanted to see Hibs victorious were at it again. This time they stoned Tom Purdie as he left the field, and somebody managed to cripple him with a kick. The police intervened and arrested a man whose name was, not surprisingly, O'Reilly.

Yet again the Hibernian support had targeted Purdie, and it took the intervention of the Hibernian players, led by captain Michael Whelahan, who gathered round their Hearts counterparts to cool the ire of their own supporters. Mr O'Reilly was fined £1 or offered ten days in prison as punishment, and Father Hannan wrote a letter of apology to Tom Purdie; yet again the Hibernian supporters had brought 'ill-fame' upon their club.

The replay took place in Corstorphine, an outlying village to the west of the city, and a crowd of 'several thousand' turned up, some of them coming on special trains that were put on for the occasion, another indicator of how the 'needle rivalry' had gained the attention of the public. Hibernian won what seems to have been a more sedate and less controversial replay 2-0, the goals coming from Whelahan and forward Frank Rourke. The Hibernian support celebrated the win 'in such an uncontrolled manner as ever witnessed at a football match in Scotland'; it was the club's first ever trophy win.

Hearts' revenge came quickly, as the rivals met again in the semi-final of another of the local competitions, the Edinburgh FA President's Cup, with Hearts winning 1-0. Little of this match appears to have been reported, other than the crowd, which was given at 2,500, again large for the times, and further proof of the pulling power of the two leading local clubs whose antipathy towards one another was increased yet further by their next meeting, a Scottish Cup third-round tie.

This time only three matches were required to separate the two teams, but the nature of the tie is instructive. It shows both how the level of trust between the two to act in good faith was gone, and that the levels of pettiness, even spitefulness, had risen considerably.

Hearts, who still had not put down roots in Gorgie at this point, were having trouble with their lease agreement for the Powderhall ground situated to the north of the city centre and which was also used by Hibernian before they secured their new home. The first match was postponed for a week due to the dispute, and then the following week Hearts were forcibly removed by the police at the behest of the owner. These two postponements led to the SFA ordering the match to go ahead at Mayfield, which was then Hibernian's home pitch, therefore stripping Hearts of their home advantage. Hearts were unhappy at this turn of events and demonstrated this by turning up at the new venue at 1pm – two hours early – to find no Hibernian opponents there. Hearts kicked through the empty net to claim the tie.

Hibernian, we are told, had anticipated such a misunderstanding and so in the week prior had placed an advert in the local papers to confirm that the match would go ahead on that day, at that venue, but at 3pm. And so when they turned up two hours later there was no Hearts, and they also kicked through the empty net and claimed the tie.

Again, the truth of the matter will never be known, but Hibernian were so sure that something like this would happen that they had arranged a back-up fixture, and so instead they played St Bernard's in an Edinburgh Cup match. According to Lugton:

> The SFA met on the following Tuesday to discuss this protracted problem. Hearts had now failed to play on three different dates and Hibernian should really have been awarded the tie, but this would have been too much to expect from the

SFA – they ordered that the match be played at Mayfield on Saturday 15th November.

Hibernian were upset, and didn't miss the opportunity to stick the boot into Hearts – this time the advert placed in the newspaper by them explicitly stated that 'in the event of Hearts failing to appear on the ground at the hour appointed by the SFA', a challenge match would take place between Hibernian and South Western – with a kick-off time of 3.10pm. Hearts did appear and the match proceeded with predictable controversy. With the tie poised at 2-1 to Hibernian, a third goal was 'scored' but disallowed. Hibernian claimed a Hearts supporter had kicked the ball back out of the goal, but the referee disagreed. This led to the Hibernian supporters invading the pitch in anger at the perceived injustice, with the police taking ten minutes to gain control and allow the match to continue, with no further goals, and Hibernian took the tie.

It was again in the Edinburgh Cup, this time a semi-final, that the two clubs would resume hostilities on the last day of January 1880, just a couple of months on from their Scottish Cup falling-out. Another large crowd, of 3,500, turned up, and they were treated to quite the match. Hearts quickly established a two-goal lead with the wind at their backs and dominated their rivals, who could barely get out of their own half. In what must have been one of the earliest examples of that oh-so famous football cliché, Hibernian completely turned it around in the second half, scoring five unanswered goals and winning through to the final to defend their Edinburgh Cup title.

'It was a lively game all through,' Mackie tells us, 'with a good deal of lusty cheering, as well as much hissing and growling, on the side-lines.'

The turnaround was credited by Hearts sources as being due to having the strong wind at their backs, and by Hibernian sources as being roared on by their fanatical supporters. Regardless, it was the biggest victory ever between the two sides, and burnished Hibernian's credentials as the dominant club in the east. Reid states: 'Broadly speaking, the "green" was above the "red" for many long years, and the Hearts attained their celebrity as the outcome of enterprise – some of it misdirected – rather than because of prowess on the field.'

The 'misdirected enterprises' hint at the strength of the rivalry, and Hearts, unable to better the Irish upstarts from the Cowgate on the field, moved to the Edinburgh FA committee rooms.

It was 8 September 1880, and the 1880/81 season had just kicked off. At a hotel in Cockburn Street, a winding passage that leads down from the Royal Mile to Edinburgh's main train station, a meeting of the Edinburgh FA took place. The Hibernian delegation didn't have far to walk from their homes in Little Ireland, which lay at the other side of the Royal Mile, and as current holders of the Edinburgh championship title, it's fair to assume that they wouldn't have anticipated that they were about to walk into an ambush, as described by Lugton:

[Hearts] put forward a motion demanding the expulsion of Hibernian from the association on the grounds of brutal play and the unruly behaviour of their supporters. Michael Whelahan and Tom O'Reilly, the Hibernian delegates at the meeting, were stunned, having of course received no prior warning of what was to come.[9]

The motion very nearly succeeded. Indeed, such was the continuing hostility towards Hibernian that ten members supported the motion, ten voted against it and five members abstained. Despite only ten of 25 members voting for Hibernian, it was enough to see Hearts' motion fail by a single vote; that's how close Hibernian came to being expelled from organised football in Edinburgh and the great Edinburgh Derby not even getting past its sixth year. So, what was behind the move?

The charge of rough play does have some grounding in the contemporary reports of the time, and Hibernian were noted for the strength of their 'charging' in those early years, although that would have been far from unusual. The charge against their fans seems much more feasible given what had been seen from them. Again, though, as Andy Mitchell pointed out, crowd trouble was not unusual in those early days of football. But while sensibilities and crowd control have to be understood in the context of the 1800s, it does seem that Hibernian had a particularly fanatical support with a propensity to riotous behaviour and violence. No doubt this perception would have helped to influence, and been influenced by, the stereotypes of drunken and unruly Irish.

To the rest of 'respectable' Edinburgh, it is maybe not so much of a leap to see that in trying to establish the fledgling game, both in the hearts and minds of the Edinburgh public and enough to gain the respect of the west coast, clubs would have viewed the hooliganism as a threat. Given that Hearts had been involved more than most, not least the multiple attacks on their captain Tom Purdie, it is perhaps not a surprise that they, as the club injured most by this hooliganism, would react the strongest.

Equally though, it's hard to ignore the fact that it was Hearts who led the charge against Hibernian. Hearts, the club whose ambitions were being directly and increasingly thwarted by this team from a despised minority, who were becoming increasingly successful, at their expense. However, that only ten of the 25 votes were cast in favour of Hibernian shows that Hearts were not alone in being annoyed and wanting rid of the greens. Whether there was merit in the grievances, or whether it was a lot of clubs resentful of the on-field success of these Irishmen, we will never know for sure.

We know through the work of numerous historians that the Irish community of Little Ireland in Edinburgh was a violent place, often blighted by drunkenness. It was home to a maligned and ignored minority, many of whom came to escape famine – something unimaginable to us today in the UK – and who on managing to escape starvation had succeeded only in finding hatred, extreme poverty and squalor in a cramped and alien city, in an alien country. One of the main reasons that Father Hannan had created a football team was to give the young men of the district a healthy pursuit to keep them away from sinful temptations like alcohol.

It is not a huge stretch, therefore, to understand that Victorian Edinburgh would have viewed these wretched individuals and their threatening religious beliefs with fear and mistrust. And then we can begin to understand how the football team that prominently represented them – and even worse, that was championing and celebrating them and winning at the expense of 'Scottish' clubs – would have been similarly feared and mistrusted, particularly when their supporters lived up (or lived down) to the negative stereotypes and expectations.

It's also worth remembering that all of this took place just five short years after Hibernian were refused entry to the Edinburgh FA on the grounds that they were Irish and not Scottish. It is unrealistic to think that the attitudes behind that decision would not have still been prevalent five years later. In fact, the memory of this blatant discrimination is still alive today, and it is not unusual for it to be brought up by Hibernian fans as evidence of the bias against the club almost 150 years later. As is discussed elsewhere, anti-Catholicism and anti-Irishness (the two are often conflated) remained a feature of Scottish society for many decades after this, and of Scottish football to this day, and so it's not a huge surprise that such views were prevalent within Victorian football. To take a more positive look, the fact that Hibernian – by the skin of their teeth – survived this attempt is perhaps testament to the more accepting and enlightened views that existed among just enough people within Edinburgh football.

From a Hibernian view, though, this violent behaviour was them defending themselves. From the very earliest days of organised football in Edinburgh they had had to literally fight for their place. When gangs would attack them at the East Meadows to keep the much-in-demand pitches free for 'Scottish' teams, it took the intervention of these same fans, toughened up by their days spent in the hardest manual labouring jobs, to show up and guard by force Hibernian's place. In the committee rooms of both the EFA and the SFA, Hibernian had been blocked on account of their nationality and religion. Their fans were convinced that they were constantly on the wrong end of discriminatory decisions, both on-field and off-field, designed to hamper them and 'keep them in their place'. Who could blame them for being a bit suspicious of an establishment, a large part of whom had made it clear that they literally did not want Irish Catholics to be involved?

Hibernian were also actively political, being prominent supporters of, and agitators for, the cause of Irish home rule, one of the main and most contentious political questions of the day in the UK. Again, context is important here. Victorian UK was at its imperial peak, the major power in the world at the head of the largest empire the world had ever seen. Scottish nationalism was in its infancy in this age of 'North Britain', where loyalty to Queen and country was valued so highly. And yet Hibernian supported and gave succour to the separatists who were challenging this power and the UK's right to possess Ireland and its people. From the 21st-century perspective, it is difficult to understand just how contentious this would have been to the sensibilities of Victorian Scotland.

Then there was the fact that these outsiders were beginning to flex their muscles considerably on the park. Lugton, the historian of Hibernian's early years, was convinced that the move was motivated by envy and dislike at the prominent position and success Hibernian had achieved so quickly. Hibernian had just won their second consecutive Edinburgh Cup, and their second XI had won the reserve team equivalent, indicating the depth of playing talent at their disposal. They were now starting to make inroads to the Scottish Cup, effectively representing east of Scotland football on the national stage. And indeed, Hibernian would go on to become the first team from the east of Scotland to make the Scottish Cup Final, and subsequently the first team to win it when they beat Dumbarton 2-1 in 1887.

And so it is also fair to assume that some involved in the vote that night were motivated out of good old self-interest, which after all remains one of the main drivers in football to this day. It is likely that at least some of the calculations behind those voting to expel Hibernian and behind Hearts' motivations for bringing the motion (and presumably lobbying their counterparts behind the scenes to support it) was simply to remove a notable competitor; a theme the Edinburgh Derby would return to a century later. It wouldn't have been lost on their rivals that Hibernian had a captive support, having no natural rivals to tempt their Irish Catholic supporters away. This was not the case for Hearts (or the other Edinburgh clubs) at the time, who were competing with one another for their support. And while Hearts had quickly established themselves at the top of Edinburgh football, they were still a nomadic club and so they didn't yet have the security of a big locality or a community from which to draw a loyal support, such as they would later have once they were established in Gorgie/Dalry.

Hibernian definitely had a natural advantage in this way, although obviously the nature of their club and support was an enormous disadvantage to them in many other ways, not least as they were the obvious target for discrimination. They would also have noticed that Hibernian were starting to draw a lot of interest from the Irish communities across Scotland, and notably gaining substantial support among the growing Irish community in Glasgow, something that was not an option to the other Edinburgh clubs and had the potential to put them at a severe financial disadvantage. It is likely that all of these, and perhaps more, factors were in play, and combined to make the attempt to expel Hibernian seem reasonable, necessary even, to Hearts and the other clubs who supported their attempt.

However, their large support was likely Hibernian's saviour, as were their needle matches with Hearts, because they were able to draw large crowds, which meant generating money. And Hibernian were increasingly a big attraction to clubs all over Scotland, and soon the north of England, because their presence always attracted a large support of local Irish keen to see the men representing their homeland in their proud green jerseys. Hibernian were box office, and they were helping – along with others like Hearts, of course – to establish the game here in Edinburgh.

The fact that the needle matches had attracted such press interest and drawn such crowds could not have been lost on the administrators of both the game and the clubs, and it would seem fair to assume that Hearts benefitted by being seen to be the 'Scotch' club who were going head-to-head with these Irish upstarts. Success breeds success, and the more successful Hearts were, the more likely they would be to attract supporters, particularly those who enjoyed seeing the Irish put back in their place. This is not to say that Hearts courted an anti-Catholic support – there is no evidence of that at all – but rather they came to be seen as among the best of the 'local' or 'Scottish' clubs.

Such an idea can only go so far though, and as the game in Scotland established itself more and more, the impetus to be the number one club in the east must have been irresistible, and so there was a quandary for Hearts. At what point does a rivalry that is useful in helping to establish them as one of the main clubs in the east, of getting them press attention and success, start to become a barrier to them in reaching their full potential? According to Mackie the next match between the clubs was a tipping point.

Hearts' ambition was clear, but their quest to become top dogs in Edinburgh did not go to plan. Mackie reproduced a letter written on behalf of the Hearts committee to two former players now playing professionally in England:

> I have been requested by the committee to see if you … would come down and play against the Hibs next Saturday, it is a cup-tie and we would like to have the team as strong as possible … I am sure you both would be made heartily welcome, and would receive the thanks of all the football followers – if we could just snuff out the Hibs.

The letter goes on:

> It is all the cry in Edinburgh just now, 'Get your men from Lancashire and for any sake beat the Hibs, let it cost what it will.'

In a match noted for lots of 'going for the man instead of the ball', Hibernian were victorious; 'Hearts were finding it hard to get Hibs off their backs.'

Hibernian – who were in the midst of a run of eight Edinburgh FA Cups/Edinburgh Shield victories in nine years (losing the other to Edinburgh University by default after Hibernian couldn't field a team due to illness) – also 'rubbed salt in the wound' with their Scottish Cup success.

Such was Hearts' striving that in 1884 they were expelled from the SFA for professionalism. While there is a general acceptance that Hearts were far from the only club indulging in the habit, they had been caught making illegal payments to players. To gain reinstatement, they had to sack the offending players and change their entire board: 'Let it cost what it will' had been taken a bit too literally. Professionalism was eventually introduced, a vindication of sorts for Hearts, but it was too late and the damage had been done.

However, their on-field fortunes were improving, and the first signs of that improvement came when they beat Hibernian in the final of the Rosebery Cup (this final running to two replays). Mackie states, 'Hearts had had enough of "taking it" from their "dear enemy" after Hibernian's Scottish Cup triumph, and in their next cup match, Hearts drew with the holders, and then beat them at Hibernian Park in the replay in what is described as Hearts' "greatest triumph in the history of the two clubs so far".' Hearts had started to turn the tables just in time to capitalise on Hibernian's implosion: 'It was the end of the beginning for Hearts and the beginning of the end for Hibs.' How that 'end' would arrive was to catch everyone off-guard.

CHAPTER 4

FALL AND RISE

1888–1907

'GO AND do likewise.'

These words, spoken with great gusto in a church hall in the East End of Glasgow, would prove to be among the most fateful ever uttered by a Hibernian official. It is a sad irony that in the moment of Hibernian's greatest triumph are to be found the seeds of their downfall; both as the club of the Irish Catholic population of Scotland and as the top team in Edinburgh.

The words were spoken by John McFadden, the secretary of Hibernian, at a reception held in the heart of the Irish community of Glasgow, to celebrate the club's triumph in the Scottish Cup of 1887, where they defeated Dumbarton 2-0. For this was not just the first time that a club from the east of Scotland had won the national competition, it was a 'triumph in which all of Scotland's Catholic Irish shared'.[10]

The rest, as they say, is history. Hibernian supported their Glasgow brethren to set up a new club, which at one point was to be called Glasgow Hibernian but, ironically, some of the new club's committee felt the name to be 'too Irish' and not sympathetic enough to their Scots–Irish identity. And so Celtic was chosen instead as a name that could appeal to Scots and Irish alike. Helping out other clubs was not unusual for Hibernian at the time; their charitable ethos and missionary zeal led to them helping birth at least 63 other Irish clubs, 38 of which used the name Hibernian along with the name of their town. In many ways it shows how little Hibernian worried about creating competitors, either because they didn't see on-field success as their main aim, or because they were hopelessly naive; it was probably a bit of both. In their defence, Hibernian were run by a priest, and so there can be no doubt about his belief that living to serve a higher purpose mattered. It wasn't just Canon Hannan, however; their captain Michael Whelahan agreed. At a St Patrick's Day reception in the Cowgate, according to Lugton, captain Michael Whelahan remarked that 'Hibernian are pledged to become the best in the country, not for personal glory, but to increase the charitable works of the Catholic Young Men's Society (CYMS) and to give a real sense of pride to all of Ireland's exiled children in Scotland.'

Unfortunately for them, their Celtic counterparts didn't see things the same way, and from the outset the new club set out to avoid what many of their committee obviously saw as the mistakes and excesses of Hibernian. They were unashamedly 'professional' (in as much as clubs could be in the days of amateurism) in their approach; in Campbell & Woods' history of Celtic, they describe how their recruitment 'had a touch of piracy about it'. That might be an understatement, because in the Celtic team that won the Scottish Cup there were half a dozen players who would have otherwise been turning out for Hibernian.

The glory of Hibernian's Scottish Cup victory in 1887 is impossible to overstate. Early football was very localised, just as life in Victorian Scotland was. The local competitions, which are now often excluded from records as 'uncompetitive', were the bread and butter of football, the domestic football of the time that sustained clubs, especially before the advent of the Scottish league. The Scottish Cup was more akin to the Champions League now, a magical competition that all dreamed of winning, while few ever did; and it was the de facto Scottish championship until the league was set up in 1890 (the Scottish Cup retained a prestige that matched the league, similarly to how the FA Cup in England did, something which has only fairly recently started to change with the increased importance of the Champions League and the money that comes from European competitions). Taking the Scottish Cup away from the early powerhouses of the west of Scotland was a major moment for the rest of Scottish football, and no mean feat. This was still the era of the mighty Queen's Park after all, who to this day remain the third-most-successful club in Scotland behind Celtic and Rangers in terms of Scottish Cup victories. Before returning to the Cowgate in Edinburgh with the trophy, Hibernian stopped for a victory dinner in the East End of Glasgow to celebrate with their Glasgow supporters. It was here, in the halls of

St Mary's Church in The Calton district (an area closely associated with Irish immigrants and within sight of what is now Celtic Park), that myth takes over.

The Hibernian version of what came next is varied and wrapped up in myth and self-pity. Hibernian played a benefit match for Celtic and supported them, and then Celtic used that money to recruit half of Hibernian's team, after John McFadden from the Hibernian committee had encouraged them 'to go and do likewise' and create a version of Hibernian in the East End of Glasgow.

Celtic's official history doesn't actually vary too much at this point, other than to attribute John McFadden's encouragement to part of an address he gave to the whole hall. Looking back at the different accounts, it seems like, as with much in football, there is no absolute truth, only different perspectives on the same event. What is not disputed is that Hibernian encouraged the fledgling Celtic, and were the active inspiration to them, so much so that the first circular issued by Celtic, in January 1888, announcing the formation of the club specifically mentions Hibernian's exploits in the east of the country as being what the new club aspired to replicate. And of course Hibernian would play the inaugural match at the new Celtic Park on 8 May 1888, versus Cowlairs (a now-defunct club from the north of Glasgow). According to the official Celtic history written by former MP Brian Wilson, he notes that at a reception afterwards, the first chairman of Celtic toasted the Hibernians. John McFadden returned the honour to the hosts, toasting Celtic and remarking that 'it would be a sorry day indeed for the Irish in Scotland when residents of one city should act in an unfriendly way towards those of another'.

Celtic did sign a raft of both Hibernian players and players Hibernian were about to sign, showing their willingness to engage in 'piracy'. Was this against the spirit of the two clubs' relationship up to this point? It probably was, but the victim narrative spun by Hibernian fans is as much about how history has played out subsequently as it is about what happened at that time. Celtic were from the start clear-eyed about their vision; creating a winning football team, and the involvement in their committee of local businessmen gave them a more cut-throat view. Equally, this was the time before contracts and wages, and the truth is many of Hibernian's players were based in the west of Scotland anyway (usually they came through smaller Irish clubs, which Hibernian had used as their feeder clubs since their inception). Being given the opportunity to play more locally, with a few financial sweeteners thrown in, wouldn't have been that difficult a decision.

Hibernian, for their part, had an equally clear-eyed view of their mission, and it was first and foremost about charity and politics, with the football club a vehicle for those aims. This was no ruthless committee with a hard business edge like Celtic; this was a church club, who donated all their money to charity, who refused to pay players, and who would only play players who were practising Catholics. Hibernian were not the innocent victims the historical narrative sometimes suggests, because Hibernian were making a conscious choice as to the kind of club they wanted to be. This is reflected in the seemingly muted response of Hibernian to this whole affair.

They were determined not to fracture the solidarity of the Irish in Scotland by causing a big fuss; although their fans made their anger clear when Celtic visited Hibernian at Hibernian Park for the first time, in October 1888, and were given a hostile reception by the home crowd; Celtic brushed it off and won 3-0 in what was a sign of things to come.

What clearly does irk Hibernian supporters to this day is the way in which history – and Celtic, with their enormous support, huge wealth and incredible sway and influence in the media – have spun this episode to reflect their own self-image as the underdog champions of the Irish in Glasgow. While this is true to an extent – they did have charitable aims – as Celtic's official club history points out, 'Celtic's charitable function [was seen] as the by-product of creating a successful, well-organised and inclusive club'; a subtle but important difference to their Edinburgh counterparts. Brother Walfrid may have a statue outside Celtic Park, but he was not the president of the new club – that honour fell to a local businessman called John Glass; Walfrid's position was an honorary one. In other words, this was a football club focused on success first, and a charitable champion of their community second. Celtic maintained this business-first approach as one half of the world-famous Old Firm – so named because of the way Celtic and Rangers worked together over the decades (implicitly and explicitly) to foster mutual antagonism and rivalry, in order to maintain and maximise income and their place at the top. Today, Celtic are a plc whose legal duty and purpose is to maximise profits for its shareholders, which include billionaires and investment companies.

A good judge of how controversial the actions were can be seen by the reaction to it from a chunk of those involved in Celtic in the early days. There were disputes within their ranks as to their direction. According to Wilson, some felt Celtic should follow Hibernian as a charitable, exclusively Catholic organisation. But the Celtic committee decided from the start not to limit itself in terms of support or players to Catholics only and eventually a split occurred. The breakaway Celtic men first of all tried to convince Hibernian to move to the East End of Glasgow and take up their hard-earned place as champions of the Irish Catholic community. When this move never materialised, they formed their own club in the East End instead. And what did they call it? Well of course they called it Glasgow Hibernian, and laid it out on the charitable path of (Edinburgh) Hibernian that Celtic had so pointedly chosen to avoid. This rival club was short-lived, as Celtic, with their relentless focus on building a winning team, quickly achieved success, and the fate of the other Irish clubs in Scotland, including Hibernian, was sealed; even if it took them decades to accept the fact.

Celtic were ruthless, but Hibernian were also feckless. They hadn't saved any money from their huge success (their ethos after all was to give it all away) and this left them totally unprepared for the coming days of professionalism. But while Celtic weakened them, and provided serious competition to them, it might not have proved as grievous a blow as it became had it not been for some concurrent bad luck, and bad faith. Their leader and founder Canon Hannan died, a huge blow to the club, and around the same time a club official disappeared with club funds to Canada. Hibernian had been hit with numerous blows, and as they staggered around like a heavyweight boxer about to be knocked out, the corner threw in the towel. Hibernian withdrew their teams, so that they could regroup and sort out their books, which had not been properly maintained. The less charitable view is that they knew their books wouldn't pass muster with the new era of professionalism and so withdrew rather than submit to scrutiny and embarrassment. How Hibernian would have been able to operate in the professional age is also a valid question, and there was surely a chance they would have faded away into their principles in the same way that the giants of Queen's Park did.

With the champions of Edinburgh toppled – ironically by a Glasgow club – the path was clear for someone else to fill that void, and Hearts were both willing and had the makings of the team to do it. They also had the infrastructure, a point made by historian Andy Mitchell, which helped them to stand out from the crowd in those early days. They moved to (first) Tynecastle Park in 1881, and due to building works were forced to relocate to the other side of the road to (current) Tynecastle Park in 1886.

The creation of the Scottish Football League in 1890 was an opportunity that Hearts were able to capitalise on. Hibernian had stopped playing while they sorted out their internal mess, and St Bernard's were also disqualified by the SFA for professionalism. In 1891, Hearts won their first Scottish Cup, defeating Dumbarton 1-0, and in 1895 Hearts won their first league championship flag, alongside the Rosebery Charity Cup and the Edinburgh League championship. Hearts then followed that up by defeating a resurgent Hibernian in the only Scottish Cup Final to ever be played outside of Glasgow. It was March 1896 and the pair met at Logie Green, then home of St Bernard's. Mackie tells us:

> As for the game it came well up to expectations. For the first seventy minutes the struggle was magnificent. The football seems to have been of an unusually high standard. But the game was said to have degenerated in the last twenty minutes, and for this the Hibs were blamed. Unlike the Hearts, who kept up to the end their finest form and their determination to play football till the final whistle, the Hibs could not produce that grand finishing spurt for which they had made something of a reputation, so that the match lost the interest of a well-matched tussle in these later stages.

Hibernian may have been back from their enforced hiatus, but Hearts were now a different beast from the one they had encountered previously and they deserved to win, and had prepared to do so – supposedly undertaking special training, and staying in a hotel for three weeks.

Hearts, with a young Bobby Walker emerging into their first team (who would go on to earn a record 29 Scotland caps), followed up the Scottish Cup triumph by winning the league championship for the second time, in 1897, pipping rivals Hibernian by two points and Rangers by three. And as the new century dawned, Hearts scored what must be their least likely triumph yet, in 1901 – an unremarkable Hearts team, struggling in the league and finishing only four points above relegation, managed to conquer Celtic 4-3, despite their Glasgow opponents chasing the title. The victory would have been made all the sweeter by them knocking out Hibernian on the way to the final after a replay. Hibernian came back the next year, and in 1902 they matched their rivals by also defeating Celtic in the final, held at Celtic Park due to Hampden being out of action. For Hibernian it was an important moment, getting back to the top of Scottish football after their travails, and doing so by beating Celtic must have been particularly satisfying. Hibernian would go on to clinch their first ever league championship in 1903 (Hearts made the Scottish Cup Final again, this time losing to Rangers). The 'Edinburgh enthusiasts' were treated to another final in 1906 when Hearts again made it; this time they beat Third Lanark 1-0 to win the Scottish Cup for the fourth time in just 16 years. Despite Hearts struggling financially after a significant outlay on a new stand, the team were still performing on the pitch. However, the debts became so unmanageable that Hearts folded the company and created a new plc, fronted by a group of businessmen who injected some new funds, including the proprietor of the *Edinburgh Evening News*, one of the main daily newspapers in the city; the club of the Edinburgh establishment indeed.

The fans of both clubs could have been forgiven for thinking the sunlit uplands of success were waiting for them. Hearts had won six major trophies in 16 years, and Hibernian, despite their fall, had recovered to claim both the league and the cup. And while the Old Firm were strong, even the most pessimistic couldn't have foreseen how dominant they were about to become, and the two old rivals from Edinburgh looked well set to seriously challenge them.

CHAPTER 5

ORIGINS

IT'S A drizzly, autumn evening as we walk into the old church and take our seats. It's hard to tell if this is still an actual church, or if it has long since been converted, as a venue for Festival shows; Edinburgh used to be full of the former, and it is now very well stocked in the latter. An historic obsession with religion, and the insatiable demand for venues for the world's largest arts festivals, have made for a happy coincidence. This one, on George IV Bridge in the Old Town, is brightly lit, furnished slightly more luxuriously than your average Presbyterian would be comfortable with, and most importantly to us on this dreich evening, it is warm.

I'm with my father-in-law, and we both take our seats halfway up the aisle. I'm suddenly aware that I am, by a long stretch, the youngest person in this congregation. The Edinburgh Historical Society, whose meeting this is, seems to have its core membership firmly in the retired demographic. Neither me nor my father-in-law are members, but I saw this event advertised and it grabbed my interest: '1827 – the world's first football club'. In Edinburgh? How come I've never heard about this before?

The talk, by football historians Andy Mitchell and John Henderson, turns out to be something of a revelation. I'm transfixed as Mitchell explains how a new archive of one John Hope, a notable Victorian worthy (another commodity of which Edinburgh is well stocked), had been relatively recently discovered. Within the archive, among other things, were written records setting out his interest and leading role in football; so far, so uncontentious. However, the English like to claim ownership over the origins of football, and Sheffield FC like to style themselves as 'the world's first football club' and their home ground as 'The Home of Football'. And yet, here is clear evidence of early Association football rules (even if they weren't yet known as that), distinct from the general mishmash of football-like games that have existed for centuries in Scotland, and from which both soccer and rugby sprang. This football club, simply called 'the Foot-Ball Club' (presumably because there wasn't another one that they had to differentiate themselves from), dates from 1824 – a full 33 years before Sheffield FC came into existence, and includes what he claims to be the first set of written rules, from 1833, 24 years before Sheffield FC saw the light of day.

Mitchell went on to explain how this was not unusual, and that Edinburgh can also claim to be home of the first (association) football medal (1851), the first inter-school match (1858) and the first organised girls' match (1861), as Mitchell and Henderson point out in their book. Given this apparent early love of football, it follows that men educated in Edinburgh – whose love of the game may well have been sparked during their time in the city – were present at the creation of the (English) Football Association in 1863. And while it is association football in which we are interested here, the mutual roots of football and rugby are impossible to ignore, and Edinburgh played host to the world's first ever rugby international, between Scotland and England in 1871 at Raeburn Place, in the Stockbridge district of the city (that pitch remains the home of the Edinburgh Academical Rugby Club to this day). Edinburgh's love for, and pioneering role in, sports didn't stop at football and rugby. Contrary to modern marketing slogans, Edinburgh – or more specifically, Leith Links – is the home of golf.

I was amazed. How come a story like this was so unknown? How had Edinburgh's place in football been lost? Overshadowed by England and its monopolising of football's early heritage, and by Glasgow, home to both the legendary pioneers Queen's Park FC and subsequently the inescapable force of the Old Firm who suck in most of the gravity, leaving the rest of Scotland's national game orbiting around them like so much cosmic debris. And yet, standing in front of me is a football historian putting Edinburgh, if not at the very centre of football's origins, then certainly much closer to the centre than anyone ever has before. I bought myself and my father-in-law a copy of their book as we left, and I started reading it as soon as I got home. The book explains how the Foot-Ball Club were a product both of their time, but also of Edinburgh itself. And as I read,

I couldn't help but notice the parallels with contemporary Edinburgh football clubs, which in some cases Mitchell makes explicitly.

Mitchell surmises that the unique characteristics of the city played a role in the development of Hope's Foot-Ball Club. The city's Old Town was home to the High School of Edinburgh, the school of choice for the city's numerous monied and storied families, of which the Hopes were one. The tightly packed urban setting meant that there were no playing fields, and so a game needed to be devised that would fit in the concrete school yard, and presumably require more upright play than rugby.

The Hope story plays into the stereotypes of Edinburgh as a genteel, middle-class city, and in many ways it is; that certainly helped create the sporting interest in those early years. Hope himself was from an aristocratic Edinburgh family that has at least seven city streets named after them,[11] as is one of the main entrances to the Royal Botanic Gardens in Edinburgh (John Hope Gateway, named after his grandfather, a famous botanist). Young men of wealth, who had leisure time and were reasonably fit, were a prerequisite, and it is notable how much of Association football's development was driven by aristocrats for this reason; time to play was a commodity available only to those with wealth. This idea of 'posh' Edinburgh has over the years helped to feed the sense that this is not a football city, but to categorise Edinburgh in such a simplistic way misunderstands the very nature of the city itself.

* * *

Edinburgh is a difficult city to write about. Not because there is nothing to say, but because there is a glut, and it has all been said before; often by some of the greatest thinkers and writers in history. It has played backdrop to fiction for hundreds of years, it features heavily in history books, and many literary greats have visited or chosen it as their home. In fact, Edinburgh was the world's first UNESCO City of Literature, and Edinburgh's most prestigious street, Princes Street, is home to the largest monument to an author anywhere in the world, the Scott Monument (built to honour Walter Scott). From the top of the Scott Monument, you can look down at the huge, glazed roof of Waverley Station, the only train station in the world to be named after a novel, Scott's *Waverley* (there are also two pubs called The Waverley in Edinburgh, as well as others named after Scott characters or novels). Scott's *Waverley* became a series of novels, the seventh of which is called *The Heart of Midlothian*.

Edinburgh may not be famous for its football, but that doesn't mean the two exist separate from one another. Edinburgh is a major protagonist in this story because it is impossible to look at the Edinburgh Derby in isolation from the city that birthed the rivalry, and has played host, backdrop, even provocateur, ever since. Edinburgh's quirks and sensibilities, its nature, its character (good and bad) and its history had, and continue to have, a profound effect on its football clubs. So, to understand the Edinburgh Derby, you have to have an understanding of the city.

Like most cities, Edinburgh has multiple personalities; there is the nice, twee, tourist-friendly face that most visitors see. This face is no less authentic than the others. Edinburgh is a stunning city, with unique historical features and sights that are absolutely part of its fabric. Edinburgh Castle is no less authentic because it is Scotland's top tourist attraction. But there is also the city away from that, the city of everyday life, of workplaces, of schools, of pubs; its inner suburbs, some of which are home to sprawling multi-million-pound Georgian and Victorian mansions; some of which are home to pile-'em-high, pack-'em-in 19th-century workers' tenements. Then there are the city's housing schemes (large, inter-war housing estates), many of which lie on the edge of the city, well out of sight of the tourists. The Glaswegian comedian Kevin Bridges once joked that Edinburgh has its rough areas, it just hides them behind mountains, a reference to Craigmillar and Niddrie, two of the city's most economically deprived areas which sit on the other side of Arthur's Seat from the city centre; Arthur's Seat itself, in the shadow of which nestles Easter Road stadium, is a huge extinct volcano that sits in the middle of Edinburgh, and which the city has wrapped itself around as it has grown. And these areas are no more or less authentic either. Edinburgh is all of these places and more, and they all contribute to the story of the city, and to the story of the football clubs that call it home.

For the people who live there, Edinburgh is where we work, raise our families, got into trouble as kids, make a living as adults. As with all homes, it is a place of both joy and melancholy; and Edinburgh wears both with equal comfort. If the long, bright northern summer evenings, when the tourists throng her streets, the world arrives for her festivals and the pubs and restaurants are full, represents her joyous side, then those dark northern winter afternoons, when the sun dips below the horizon before 4pm and cloaks the city in the fading light of the gloaming, represent her prosaic side; the side she keeps for us, her inhabitants. And as glorious as the city is in the high summer sunshine, so she suits just as well the half-light of short winter days, when the air is cold, clear and crisp, and your breath puffs out in front of you like the steam from an old locomotive. This dour, understated side of Edinburgh's personality is the one which serves as a backdrop to the football season as it runs through the winter.

In his book *The Strange Case of Dr Jekyll and Mr Hyde*, Robert Louis Stevenson brought to life the contradictory nature of Edinburgh in the titular character (or characters?). The story was inspired by a real-life Edinburgh personality, William Brodie, a deacon of the city who by day lived as a respectable citizen, but who by night led a secret double life as a burglar. Deacon Brodie is today immortalised with the highest honour that can be bestowed upon a Scot – he has a pub named after him, Deacon Brodie's Tavern, which sits proudly on the Royal Mile and, ironically, right opposite the High Court. Stevenson understood Edinburgh well, and in fact he wrote a whole non-fiction piece about the city simply titled *Edinburgh: Picturesque Notes*. In this book, he explores what are to him some of the notable features of the city, good and bad. At various points and in various circumstances, both Hearts and Hibernian have represented these different sides of the city; I think Robert Louis Stevenson would have approved of the clubs.

Growing up in Edinburgh, I did not escape the literary links. My school – James Gillespie's High – was famous for educating, and possibly inspiring, Dame Muriel Spark and her classic novel *The Prime of Miss Jean Brodie*, although to the shame of my former school, I have never read it. And while Sherlock Holmes famously lived in London, he is immortalised in brass at the top of the main road from the city centre down towards Leith. Arthur Conan Doyle, his creator, sprang from the same Irish immigrant community as Hibernian and, fittingly, after a particularly unlikely League Cup triumph in 1991 Edinburgh awoke on the Monday morning to Holmes with a bottle of Beck's beer perched on top of his famous pipe, and a green and white scarf proudly around his neck. The statue stands opposite the Conan Doyle pub; Edinburgh is almost as in love with its pubs as it is with its writers and the two passions regularly collide. But the literary references aren't all old and historic either.

Harry Potter was said to have been inspired by and written in Edinburgh, and J.K. Rowling still lives in the city. I wonder if there is any significance in the school house of the eponymous hero, Gryffindor, having maroon as a colour, while its arch-enemy Slytherin wear green. If there is, Hearts fans will enjoy the fact that the maroon of Gryffindor is paired with gold while the green of Slytherin is paired with only silver. And other contemporary writers, Ian Rankin and Irvine Welsh, are both fans of Hibernian and have woven the Edinburgh Derby into their works, with their main protagonists often being Hibernian supporters. Welsh – who wrote for a Hibernian fanzine under a pen name before he achieved his success – also regularly sets his worst or most pathetic and/or perverted characters as Hearts fans. Perhaps this balances out the bias J.K. Rowling wrote into Hogwarts.

Welsh's most famous novel *Trainspotting* (and the subsequent cult classic film) gave life to the seedy underbelly of the city; drug addiction, poverty, urban wastelands and social decay, based largely on his own experiences of being born and raised in one of those large housing estates that sit on the northern edge of the city, Muirhouse. The novel is set in the 1980s when Edinburgh had the dubious title of 'heroin capital of Europe', which, given the habit of drug users to share dirty needles, quickly became the 'AIDS capital of Europe'. Fans of both Hibernian and Hearts are regularly reminded of these facts by fans of other clubs, who often refer to them as 'spoon burners' (after the process of boiling heroin down in a teaspoon to create an injectable liquid), gesture a tapping on their upturned arm (as if looking for veins into which to inject) or, in Hibernian's case, simply by referring to them as HIVs (from the HIV virus) rather than Hibs. Given the connection between *Trainspotting* and Leith, Hibernian are more closely associated with it and receive the bulk of the insults (including from Hearts supporters).

Leaving aside Welsh's club allegiance, his work is important because it was one of the first to be written in a form of Scots (the traditional dialect of the Scottish Lowlands), specifically the slang vernacular of Edinburgh. It makes the book a difficult read, and I can still remember it taking a couple of chapters to get used to reading it as it would be spoken, rather than as it is written. Once I had done that, it was something I had never encountered before. A real (and by then quite famous) book where the people sounded like the people I heard, like my family, and my parents' friends, and definitely the men I heard at the football on a Saturday afternoon. And this was part of its power. Edinburgh is no stranger to literary genius, but this was high culture that shone a light on the poorer, working (or often not working) people of the city, who spoke the dialect of the working classes, a dialect long since discarded by 'respectable' Edinburgh who had taken on the Anglo sensibilities of 'proper English'. And of course, this is the language of the football fan and to this day some of the best examples of lots of people talking loudly and authentically in this dialect can be heard in the pubs and clubs around both Tynecastle and Easter Road on a matchday.

All of this is not just mere background to the Edinburgh Derby, because just as the language of the Edinburgh working classes was invisible to many before *Trainspotting*, so was the entire working class. The Scottish media have traditionally focused on, and often fetishised, the industrial hard-man of Glasgow as the embodiment of male, working-class Scotland, and 'Glasgow patter' was often used as a synonym for Scottish patter, something that long bristled in the east of the country. Partly this was because the Scottish media is largely based in Glasgow and partly it was just sheer weight of numbers (Glasgow is Scotland's largest city). This rough-around-the-edges image remains a huge part of the identity of Glasgow and its surrounding areas today.

The absence of Edinburgh working-class culture in the Scottish media comes from the same preconception that Edinburgh is 'not a football city'. That it is instead a city of lawyers and judges and financiers, and that everyone goes to private school, then university, and watches rugby. Edinburgh is genteel and sophisticated, boring and snooty. Glasgow is salt of the earth and industrial, if a little violent. As is so often the case with such stereotypes, they are partly based in truth. Edinburgh is an affluent city full of highly educated professionals, and Glasgow is a city that has always been closely associated with urban deprivation; violence, knife crime and street gangs are very much part of its identity, and promoted as such by themselves. Ironically the industry that did exist in Edinburgh was pivotal to the development of football in the city. While Edinburgh remained a city characterised by its affluence and its professions, there were a few industries that flourished; chief among them was brewing.

When I spoke to Andy Mitchell a couple of years after his revelatory talk that night, he explained how Edinburgh, but for a couple of historical quirks of fate, was set to become the home of football as we know it. In the 1850s, two pitches existed next to each other on Raeburn Place in the city, both of which are still there today. One is now The

Grange Cricket Club, the other still in its original purpose as playing fields for Edinburgh Academical, the rugby team of the Edinburgh Academy school who are the second-oldest rugby club still in existence today anywhere in the world (and who, in a nod to the shared origins of the codes, are still called Edinburgh Academical Football Club). If a dispute on the lease had gone differently, one of those pitches would have been used for the kicking game, rather than the handling game. At the time, there was a mass of young men eager to play any version of football. Rugby was chosen, and the Edinburgh private schools followed suit, an historic quirk that is very much ingrained in middle-class Edinburgh to this day, with the city's private schools and their associated rugby clubs playing a major role in the development of the rugby game in Scotland. This cast the dye into Edinburgh society, where rugby was the middle-class sport, and Edinburgh's sporting affections would always be a bit torn between the competing codes.[12] But the football capital of Scotland would become Glasgow, as a result of the exploits and early fame of Queen's Park FC, and many others.

There is one last link between Hope, the Foot-Ball Club, and the more recognisable, modern football of Edinburgh. Hope's interests in the military led to him founding the 3rd Edinburgh Rifle Volunteer Company who, in turn, and with Hope's encouragement, would create a football team. 3rd Edinburgh Rifle Volunteers Football Club (3rd ERV) would become a founding member of the Edinburgh Football Association in 1874 and winners of the first ever Edinburgh Cup, in 1876, (presented to the winning captain by none other than John Hope himself) and pivotal to the development of the game in the east, even if 3rd ERV dwindled away over concerns that the football was getting in the way of their military purpose. Some of their players then joined the third force of early Edinburgh football (although, despite speculation to the contrary, they do not seem to have any formal ties), St Bernard's Football Club. From the same Stockbridge district of the city where Raeburn Place sits, St Bernard's won the Scottish Cup in 1895, and held a notable, if unspectacular, place in the Scottish leagues until the late 1940s. A fragment of terracing from their old Royal Gymnasium ground is still visible in what has since become a public park in Eyre Place. Of all the monuments, remnants and links to John Hope and his family scattered around the city – and there are many – it must be the least grand; but as one of very few physical links to early Edinburgh football, it is surely the most fitting.

CHAPTER 6

FOREIGNERS IN A FOREIGN LAND

IN THE summer of 2022 a party of Hibernian supporters travelled, accompanied by a club director, to Ballingarry, a small idyllic village in County Limerick, south-west Ireland. They were there to attend a ceremony at The Paddocks, the home ground of Ballingarry AFC, to unveil a new memorial. It was a mosaic set into a stone wall, with black plaques on either side.

The mosaic is round, bright white and has a gold harp in the middle, three shamrocks on either side and the inscription 'HFC 1875'. It is an exact replica of the harps that used to be on the entrance gates to Easter Road before they were removed in the 1950s. Ballingarry is the home village of Hibernian's founder and club president Canon Edward Joseph Hannan, the parish priest of St Patrick's Church and the memorial is dedicated to his memory, preserving the link between the village and Hibernian Football Club.

Speaking to the club's own website, director Stephen Dunn said of the memorial:

It was an honour to take part in this event. As we
come to our 150th anniversary it is fitting that
we recognise those who established the Club, but
more, the work Canon Hannan did in his parish
to look after the poor. He can only be described
as a humanitarian. He also helped create a Club
cherished around the world, and for that we are
eternally grateful.

The club may have been eternally grateful to Canon
Hannan, but for reasons that remain unclear, they didn't
want to have the harp mosaic on permanent display at
Easter Road, which is why it was decided to take it to
Ballingarry. Hibernian have a strange relationship with
its club crests. The whole event was organised by the St
Patrick's Supporters' Club, a branch specifically set up to
celebrate and continue Hibernian's roots and founding
ethos of social conscience; the fan who made the mosaic
and offered it to the club was a member.

In fact Hibernian's relationship with their own identity
has been so difficult that they have changed their crest *at least*
four different times. I say 'at least', because the exact number
isn't particularly clear. There was a period from around the
1940s to the 1960s when the club used at least two new
club crests, which would bring the total to six, and there are
other informal versions that seem to have popped up over
the years. And to be clear, this isn't tweaking design points,
modernisations or variations on a theme. No, this is wholesale,
radical redesign that has zero relation to what went before it.

From its inception, the symbol of Hibernian FC was the gold harp of Ireland. When and why it was changed is where it gets difficult. According to Dr John Kelly, an academic at the University of Edinburgh who has researched identity in Edinburgh football:

> Symbolism of this type has tended to be a contentious issue for Hibs supporters. The club's badge has changed frequently over the years, reflecting an ongoing debate about the club's identity. This debate has centred on whether its Irish heritage should be proudly displayed or made inconspicuous for fear of accusations of sectarianism.

Harry Swan was a shareholder, then chairman of Hibernian FC, and in so doing became the first non-Irish Catholic to be involved in the running of the club. He was unashamedly a moderniser, which is what attracted Hibernian to him, for they were a club going nowhere with their absentee owners, the 'ould Irish shareholders'. Modernising and football are difficult concepts to get right, however. Swan altered the Hibernian strip, disposing of the old dark green and introducing a brighter green with white sleeves, in the style of Arsenal. Swan also wanted to change the club's colours to red and white, but was dissuaded from pressing ahead with this plan, a fact confirmed by Kelly in 2019. It was in this period that the harp and shamrock mosaics that adorned the Easter Road gates were removed during building work. After the building work had finished, the harps were not replaced, and around the same time a new badge, containing a thistle and with the words 'HFC Edinburgh', appeared on matchday programmes and other materials. Not even the club's name made it, just the name 'Edinburgh'.

This was of course the era of the post-war boom, and Hibernian were attracting huge crowds, most of whom would have just fought for king and country, and many of whom would have had no connection with the club's traditional support among the Irish Catholic community. Was it an attempt to ingratiate the club with a wider support? Choosing the thistle, one of the most obvious and recognisable symbols of Scottishness to replace one of the most obvious and recognisable symbols of Irishness does seem like a clear attempt to make a statement.

By the time the 1960s came along, the club had begun using a version of the Edinburgh city crest, a stylised Edinburgh Castle. Then came a fairly nondescript badge, with a football and some laurel leaves and a crown on it (similar to Real Madrid's) and this survived until a 'rebranding' exercise took place in the late 1980s under new owners. What they came up with has variously been described as a beer label, or just 'Saturn'; it was an oval shape, with a sloping bar across the front (that looked like the rings of Saturn). The club were just making it up as they went, and none of these badges showed any regard for Hibernian's heritage, nor indicated a club with any sense of who, or what, it was for.

The 'Saturn' badge was universally disliked, and it was replaced by the current incarnation in 2001, badge number six. The current crest is busy, and it encompasses the harp, the good ship *Persevere* of Leith and Edinburgh Castle. It is a compromise, but it seems to be well liked and does a good job of representing the club's support. Not everyone approved, however: Hearts historian David Speed, quoted by Kelly & Bairner, remarked, 'I notice that Hibs have put Edinburgh on their badge because they struggle for identity, as far as I am concerned, as an Edinburgh club. We consider ourselves to be the city's club. When they put Edinburgh on their badge, I thought, "Well, that's a wee bit petty."'

Do Hibernian struggle for identity as an Edinburgh club? And why would the Hearts historian find their rivals in the Edinburgh Derby, with whom they have shared a city for 150 years, 'petty' for including the name of that city on their crest? To clarify, it's not just the new badge that includes the name Edinburgh; it had been on the two previous official versions as well, which date back to the 1960s. Speed's sense of ownership on behalf of his club hints at deeper history that Hibernian were (and still are to some) outsiders in their home city; less legitimate, less authentic, less *Edinburgh*.

It may be coincidence that the removal of the Irish symbols happened at a time of surging crowds, post-war British nationalism, and a club owner who had already demonstrated (by changing the strip) that he was not in thrall to tradition. Swan was forward-thinking and determined to grow the club and the finances it could bring in. It seems entirely reasonable to conclude that he made a calculation that to grow the club beyond its traditional base of support, it would have to make the club more appealing to potential new fans; new fans not from the traditional Irish/Catholic community and who would not be attracted by an overly Irish Catholic club.

It's also worth pointing out that Hibernian in their traditional form, owned by the Irish shareholders, was the club which Swan had first joined in the 1930s, a club that was moribund and going nowhere. And while Swan could be accused of certain things – a lack of sentimentality or due reverence for the past – he certainly did not preside over a club that would go nowhere. It seems entirely likely that Swan made a conscious choice to move Hibernian away from their roots in an active play to become a more established 'Edinburgh' club with a larger core support. Not because he was anti-Irish or anti-Catholic – rumours that long dogged him, but which don't really stand up to scrutiny[13] – but instead because he was a moderniser.

Hibernian first played Hearts on Christmas Day 1875 on the Meadows in Edinburgh, and Hibernian's club rooms were for many years in St Mary's Street in the Old Town, where the club comes from and from where it drew most of its support in those early days. In playing that fixture, Hearts were actually breaking a decree by the Edinburgh FA not to play against Hibernian, on account of their religion and ethnicity. Hibernian were refused permission to play in the first Edinburgh FA Cup, as neither the Edinburgh

FA or the Scottish FA would admit them as members – a decision that some, including Hibernian historian John Mackay, lay at the door of John Hope, whose animosity towards Catholics was well known.

Swan's period in charge of the club was undoubtedly a successful one, and regardless of what you might think about his reign[14] he had a clear vision and implemented it, and that vision involved Hibernian being a success on and off the park with the Edinburgh public. And his dilution of the Irishness of the club worked, to the point that you had Hibernian fans who were not only indifferent to their past, but would even have been quite hostile to it. One interviewee recalled how their grandfather wouldn't have been very pleased if his grandchildren had been 'green grapes' – rhyming slang for 'papes', a derogatory term for Catholics. Yet he was a Hibernian fan, and from that World War Two generation.

Whether it was right that Swan sacrificed parts of the club's identity to do it is for Hibernian fans to debate (and they have been, for around half of their club's existence!). The success of his vision was spectacular but short-lived, and as 'the Famous Five' team got old and broke up, Hibernian plummeted, as did their crowds, and his reign ended with the club nowhere near the top. The seeds of Hibernian's identity crisis can be found in this period and Swan's vision; the fact that a club, who for half of their history had such a unique and rich culture and history, and were a proud symbol of a small but historically important community in Edinburgh, could get to the stage when a large proportion (how big a proportion is up for debate) would be offended by Irish flags being waved at Easter Road? In fact, it was a long-held rule that Irish flags were banned by the club from Easter Road through much of the 1980s and 90s. Kelly states:

> If you read a lot of the Hibs history books from the eighties right up until ye know, the mid to late nineties, there'll be mibee a page about how Hibs were formed by Irish immigrants moving into Edinburgh and that was it ... it's like the sort of embarrassing uncle that they keep away and they don't like to talk about.[15]

Kelly also highlights that up until 2005, when unofficial club historian Alan Lugton published the first of his books on the beginnings of Hibernian, the club website's account of Hibernian's entire off-field history amounted to a single sentence. Lugton wrote a trilogy about it; the club couldn't even manage three sentences.

> Not only is there no reference to Catholicism – exclusively Catholic players in the early days, or Canon Hannan and the CYMS's involvement – but the early difficulties encountered by the club in attempting to join the Edinburgh and Scottish FAs had been historically revised.[16]

The charge of historical revisionism chimes, particularly in light of the symbols being purged during the 50s – it is hard not to conclude that it was done deliberately and out of embarrassment or shame. Hibernian had not only been an Irish Catholic club, but they were a particularly political club, prominent in the issue of Irish nationalism. The club were founded on the birthday of Daniel O'Connell, an Irish nationalist, after whom Dublin's famous main street is named, and a range of speakers and celebrities to the cause would be invited to speak at events. Dublin's main train station is named after James Connolly, a young fan of Hibernian who was present at their founding (so the myth tells us) and who helped to lead the 1916 Easter Rising in Dublin against British rule.[17]

The political movement was so prominent it nearly caused a schism, as a senior member of the club had to leave his post on account of a disagreement with the church (who were trying to distance Catholicism from Irish nationalism). Singing political and Irish folk songs was a tradition popularised by the Hibernian support – one historian credits them with being the first support to engage in mass singing at a football match – and it is a tradition that continued well into the 1970s. And in the 1920s, Hibernian played a benefit match to aid the Catholic families in Belfast suffering due to the Irish War of Independence and subsequent civil war, a provocative act, given Britain – including many Scottish soldiers, some veterans of World War One – was actively fighting against the Irish nationalist forces. And this is really the heart of the debate around Hibernian's identity; how much, if at all, should the club be honouring or beholden to its founding history and traditions? Well, from the 1950s to the late 1990s Hibernian, it seems, tried their best to ignore, or at least minimise, them to the point of irrelevance.

In many ways this is where the Leith connection really starts to strengthen. The club's Leith identity has grown as its religious and ethnic identity has receded, becoming the club's secular identity, slowly growing in importance and official endorsement as the club moved away from anything 'too Irish'. It is a long-established identity, but it too was originally based on Leith's Irish Catholic population, although that has clearly spread over the decades. But what about Hibernian supporters who are not from Leith? 'It's another part of the Hibs dual identity that they are seen as this big Leith club and they are in many ways. Yet they come from the Cowgate and their traditional support was always from the Southside of Edinburgh which was where the Irish immigrant population lived.'[18]

Hibernian's Leith identity – which has become more prominent in recent decades – has never felt in opposition to their Irish heritage. And while different Hibernian supporters will give different levels of importance depending on theirs – or their families' – background and story, there seems to be an easy acceptance that the two can both be true at the same time. They certainly were for the Farmer family, whose Catholic and Leith backgrounds were pivotal to their respective roles in saving the club at two different points, a century apart.

The Leith identity suits Hibernian, but it also suits Hearts. It means that Hibernian's identity as the 'other', which was for decades based on religious difference, could be transferred to them being from Leith (although some Hearts supporters contend that they are not even from Leith, so are in fact from Lochend, a fairly rundown area in the east of Edinburgh). Leith has the feel of an underdog, and while it has been gentrified in recent decades, it has become young, trendy and cosmopolitan more than it has ever become posh. It is a working-class area, with a specific look and feel and a genuine sense of community.

For most football clubs, their history fades into the past within a generation or two. Decisions made decades previously are lost in the mists of time, shorn of their emotion or controversy, of their power. Think how many modern clubs are the result of mergers, and then think how many of them care about it anymore, despite merging clubs being one of the greatest taboos in football. As long as your club exists today, then you assume the decisions made in the past were the correct ones, for how can anyone ever prove otherwise? There are few clubs who have a living, breathing example of what another set of decisions might have meant, but Hibernian do have that.

Hibernian and Celtic share common ancestry, and in those early years Hibernian were more closely defined by their religion and their Irish politics than Celtic. In fact, it was sticking to their religious scruples and not embracing the inevitable march of professionalism that allowed their Glasgow progeny to steal a march and usurp them as the leading club of the Irish diaspora in Scotland. We can never know whether Hibernian would have followed the same path as Celtic and achieved the same success, but more than a few Hibernian fans must have thought about it over the years, and for decades thereafter Hibernian seemed obsessed, not by trying to become the top club in Edinburgh again, but to try and regain their place as the leading Irish club in Scotland, a fool's errand as it turned out.

* * *

There was a recent BBC Scotland hit comedy/drama called *Guilt*, which was set in Edinburgh, mostly in and around Leith (although much of it wasn't filmed in Leith). The premise was a series of far-fetched, interlocking relationships that were all knocked over like dominoes after two brothers accidentally run over an old man on their way home from a wedding. One of the brothers, Jake, is the down-on-his-luck brother, who owns a cool record shop and has an encyclopaedic knowledge of music. The character is a Hibernian fan, and there are numerous references and shots of Easter Road throughout. The real-life actor, who comes from Lochend, has 'Lochend' and a shamrock tattooed on his breast, clearly visible in one of the episodes. Lochend Shamrock is the name of the local gang in that part of Edinburgh. In a later episode, there is a Church of Scotland minister, based in a fictional Leith church, whose pinboard is adorned with pictures of the great Turnbull's Tornadoes side of the early 1970s, as well as various other tickets and programmes from Hibernian matches. The minister makes a couple of references to his dislike of the Roman Catholic faith, calling it the 'yoke of Popery'. Proud Leither, proud

Hibernian fan, actively dislikes Catholicism. The use of the word Popery is interesting too, as it conjures images of militant anti-Catholic movements of the 1930s and their 'No Popery' slogans, which often did particularly well in recruiting their followers in Leith.

Of course these characters are fictional, but they do quite neatly – and completely incidentally to the overall plot – capture the strange contradictions at the heart of the Hibernian identity, and just how much the identity of the club has been pulled in different directions. Today, it's fair to say that Hibernian's Leith connection is the strongest single component of their identity, one that the club actively tries to market and make a virtue of, at the same time as it, slightly confusingly, makes a big play to be Edinburgh's club. But such are the follies of marketing teams looking to exploit realities to create USPs and sell shirts.

* * *

There is a lively academic debate in Scotland on sectarianism, both in and out of football. One such book, *Bigotry, Football and Scotland*, states:

> Those in Scotland who view Irish symbolism pejoratively are often not anti-Irish/Ulster bigots even though their attitudes can occasionally coincide with intolerant attitudes around difference. They simply attach alternative ideological baggage to these symbols. There is a difficult balance to achieve, however. To what

extent diasporic groups abandon their cultural songs and symbols to appease wider sections of the community who often remain ignorant of some of the deeper meanings and traditions, and to what extent should the diaspora groups adapt to ensure they do not offend? This is one of the key questions ...

A key question indeed, and one that could be applied to Hibernian's struggles with its own identity, an issue with which they have been wrestling for decades.

The reasons that people become Hibbies are different and reflect the different identities of the club. In Andy MacVannan's book *We are Hibernian*, seven of the fans he interviewed cited family/their father, four cited Leith specifically, three cited Irish/Catholic identity, two cited Leith Catholic identity, one more cited a Leith/Southside identity and five had various random reasons.

Hibernian FC now sell official club merchandise in the club shop using the harp motif. While the significance of a cheap club-branded mug could easily be overstated, the fact the club sell all manner of merchandise now with a traditional harp unaccompanied by other symbols is significant. It is the first time they have ever done this. They also use the good ship *Persevere* of Leith and Leith's motto, Persevere. This became the leitmotif of Hibernian's Scottish Cup victory in 2016 – indeed one of the Hibernian supporters I interviewed had it tattooed on his chest after the cup win. The celebrations after that cup win centred around Leith Links, where an open-air carnival took place the day after, and the open-top bus parade went down Leith Walk. When Hibernian last won the cup in 1887 and 1902 the celebrations centred on the Old Town and the Cowgate. There might be a symbolism to that change of focus.

Hibernian choosing to base themselves where they did way back in the 19th century, at the top of Easter Road, meant that the club was equidistant from its two main bases of support, the Cowgate and Leith. The current Easter Road straddles the border between Edinburgh and Leith. There is definitely a symbolism to that.

CHAPTER 7

THE LOST GENERATION

1908–1918

IT MUST have been a uniquely innocent period in the history of Scottish football, and particularly for Hearts and Hibernian. Both had been on journeys, and suffered disappointments, but both had also proved that they could win, that they had it in them to take on all comers. The Old Firm, while prominent, had not yet closed their fingers around the neck of Scottish football as they would soon do, and both Edinburgh clubs had a recent history of winning. There is almost a sadness looking back at this period, as those involved couldn't have known that their best days were behind them and that what the footballing fates had in store for them was penury on the pitch, and tragedy off it.

Hibernian had a mediocre side just as war broke out, but they did manage to reach the Scottish Cup Final in season 1913/14, only to be thwarted by their progeny turned nemesis, Celtic, losing 4-1 in a replay after a 0-0 draw in the first match. Amazingly, just two days later Hibernian were again playing Celtic in Glasgow in the league, losing

3-0, a result that went a long way to securing the league title for Celtic, ironically at the expense of Hearts. This was the first in a long sequence of nine consecutive Scottish Cup Final defeats for Hibernian – running to 12 matches if replays are included, a curse that ran for 114 years. This 'all-Irish' final was noted for its overt political overtones, as the issue of Irish home rule dominated politics, with much singing of Irish songs between the two sets of supporters according to Lugton.

> This was, more or less, a last-ditch attempt to try and stem the leakage to Parkhead of the Glasgow Irish support: 'Hibernian have allowed themselves for too long now to play second fiddle to Celtic. At one time, Hibernian commanded the allegiance of every Irishman and woman in Scotland, but the decline in the Edinburgh Irishmen's fortunes and the rise of Celtic's has badly weakened the Easter Road men. After all is said and done, Hibs have no one to blame but themselves. They simply lack the ambition of Celtic.

Hibernian may or may not have been lacking in ambition; either way their lack of wealth held them back: Hibernian were poor. Their supporters were poor, and more tellingly they had a poor set of directors. Unlike their rivals, the business community didn't come to their rescue, and they stagnated. Lugton again tells us:

Hearts gates are bigger, a policy of enterprise has been paid at Tynecastle. I submit it is more than some time that some enterprise was being shown at Easter Road ... They have failed to thrill their very faithful support at their romantic Holy Ground ... In the Scottish Cup clubs in Hibs' position can dream dreams, but Hibs have not; in the last ten years it has been ever thus with the Hibernians.

The lack of ambition was obviously not winning Hibernian any friends, something Lugton attributes to the snobbishness of Edinburgh, looking down on Hibernian and its fans: 'It is no discouragement to Hibernian to say that had Hearts been in the final greater enthusiasm would prevail in Edinburgh.'[19] Another journalist added, 'Edinburgh is not unduly elated over the cup tie successes of the Easter Road side.'[20] The match ended in a 0-0 draw, Hibernian almost pinching it at the end but the ball dribbled past the post. Hibs' chances ended when they were made to play a league match the day before the final replay, and Hibernian duly returned to Ibrox Park to lose 4-1 to Celtic.

For Hearts, the beginning of World War One was a great 'what if' moment. The start of season 1914/15 saw Hearts run up eight successive victories, and a title challenge was on the cards. But their fortunes on the pitch fell away, as their entire first team left to volunteer for active service as part of 'McCrae's Battalion'. It seems trite to mention that in these circumstances, despite their falling away, they still finished a very credible second to Celtic.

The First World War's significance has dimmed as it has retreated into the mists of time and is eclipsed by its more famous sequel in 1939, but the scale of the slaughter is simply unimaginable today, and Scotland was hit disproportionately hard; in fact, only Turkey and Serbia had a higher percentage of war dead than Scotland. Of the 557,000 Scots who enlisted, 26.4 per cent were killed (the UK average of KIA was 11.8 per cent), and it hit the east of Scotland especially hard. For example, in the mining towns of Midlothian which surround Edinburgh, more than one third of miners had enlisted (which perhaps says something about what it was like to be a miner in those days). And while history has not been kind to those who instigated the conflict – it's increasingly viewed as a needless imperial slaughter of working men on the orders of indifferent aristocrats – to the men who joined up at the time, they were simply following their mates to do what they saw as their duty to Great Britain and Empire.

The impact of the war on football across Scotland was huge, and the lack of regionalisation meant that the east of Scotland teams were at a greater disadvantage given their higher travel expenses to play the majority of teams in the west of Scotland, and the high number of reserved occupations in the industrial heartlands of the west of Scotland gave them a far greater pool of talent, and supporters, to draw upon. So much so in fact, that of the 17 teams who began wartime football in 1914 from the east of Scotland, only Hearts and Hibernian remained playing by war's end. And Hibernian had become so impoverished by the lack of income that they couldn't afford a new set of strips, their green jerseys having apparently started to turn a putrid yellow due to staining and rewashing over a period of years, a source of some ridicule at the time. Hibernian's sartorial difficulties were matched on the pitch, where an 11th-place finish in season 1914/15 was followed by bottom four finishes for the rest of the war.

CHAPTER 8

EDINA'S DARLINGS

'We do consider ourselves to be a wee bit special. We do see the Hearts as a cut above the rest. I can imagine every Hibs fan cringing at me saying that, but that's how we feel. We are Edinburgh's club and the number one club in the city.'[21]

I MET Ross outside his flat in Marchmont, a trendy inner suburb of Edinburgh. Its proximity to one of the city's largest parks – The Meadows – as well as the city centre and the university has made it much sought after and in demand, with prices to match. Ironically, The Meadows is where Hearts and Hibernian played their first ever match, in 1875, and is widely credited with being the crucible in which Edinburgh's football culture was forged. Popular with students and young professionals, Marchmont is a very distinctive area, made up entirely of tall, grand tenement blocks, complete with beautiful bay windows and architectural flourishes. It was built to house the growing middle class in Victorian Edinburgh, those who were not yet rich enough to afford a grand townhouse or a country pile, but who could happily afford a fancy flat. Ross and I greet each other, then he leads the way, marching briskly as if his muscle memory has taken over, as this is the route he walks when he has a clear purpose: to get to Tynecastle to watch Hearts.

We make our way down through Merchiston, a very upper-middle-class area packed with yet more fancy tenements – Edinburgh does a very strong line in grand tenements – and enormous mansions set back from the road where doctors, surgeons and lawyers live. It's the area where Ross grew up, and he tells me how, before he was old enough to go to the matches, when he was playing in his front garden with his dog, he could hear the roars from Tynecastle if Hearts were playing at home.

It wasn't just the proximity of his upbringing to Tynecastle that led to Ross supporting Hearts, though: 'My father supported Hearts, his father supported Hearts, and my ancestors came from the Old Town, within spitting distance of the actual Heart of Midlothian. I mean, why wouldn't you support Hearts? I don't get why anyone from Edinburgh wouldn't, we are the Edinburgh team.' I turn to look at him to see if his face gives away any recognition of just how bold a statement that is to make in a two-club city, but there is no hint of a smile; he doesn't appear to be saying it with any knowing sense of exaggeration or humour. He means it; he *knows* it.

'One of the things I love about Hearts,' he tells me as we continue through Merchiston in what seems to be a long and gradual hill down to Gorgie, 'is it's 15 minutes' walk from my house, or from town – Hearts are literally central to Edinburgh.'

'What about Hibs?' I ask him. 'You could probably walk from Princes Street to Easter Road in 15 minutes too couldn't you?'

'Aye, but that's in Leith, Hibs are Leith. Who gives a fuck about Leith?'

Despite Ross's perceptions, Hearts aren't based in the city centre at all. Their home – since 1881 – is Gorgie, a distinctive area that runs in a long narrow strip away from the city along with its neighbouring district, Dalry, both of which grow out on either side of a single main road. It is one of Edinburgh's few obviously industrial areas, dominated as it was by breweries, distilleries, and their various infrastructure such as railways and Edinburgh's only canal. It is unmistakably inner city, and like Marchmont it's dominated by tall tenements. These are workers' tenements though, unfussy and plain in their design, and packed in tightly on either side of Dalry Road, which eventually becomes Gorgie Road.

To be fair to Ross, its hardly an original line. One of the club's unofficial slogans, emblazoned on merchandise and scarves, is that they are 'the heart and soul of Edinburgh', something their matchday host at the stadium shouts loudly to them before every match. Ross even has that slogan on his Hearts official merchandise coaster, just so he is reminded every time he takes a sip of tea. Not that he seems likely to forget.

The Edinburgh MP Ian Murray, Scotland's last remaining Labour MP in the UK Parliament, who was prominent in the movement to save Hearts from financial Armageddon in 2013/14, described Hearts in an interview as '*obviously* Edinburgh's premier club'.[22] And the club's own Twitter biography uses the 'Heart and Soul of Edinburgh' line.

I point out the irony of using this as a slogan at a time when Hearts are currently playing in the second tier of Scottish football after a surprising and controversial relegation the previous year, the season cut short by the coronavirus pandemic. He shrugs it off. 'It's temporary,' he tells me, again without a hint of doubt. 'The natural order will be restored soon enough ...' This time, he shoots me a knowing grin.

The term 'natural order' gained a degree of fame in 2018 when Hearts beat Hibernian 1-0 to knock them out of the Scottish Cup. It was Hearts' first derby victory in nine matches and came after two successive seasons where Hibernian had knocked them out of the Scottish Cup (the two clubs being drawn together three successive seasons was a strange coincidence rather than a regular occurrence). Hearts' then manager Craig Levein, whose derby record as both a player and manager (over two separate spells) is formidable, said in his post-match comments that the 'natural order' had been restored in the city after his side's victory.

Whether it was an off-the-cuff comment, or one deliberately designed to appeal to the Hearts support while also riling the Hibernian fans was unclear, but it doesn't really matter; it did both. It also provided an insight into the sense of certainty among Hearts and their fans that they are indeed the 'heart and soul of Edinburgh'. Like the club he represented and managed with such distinction, he was revealing complete confidence as to their place in the world, and their world is Edinburgh; *their* city.

As we progress down Yeaman Place, the line of tenements is broken by the Union Canal, which runs through this district in a long straight line, confirming the industrial heritage through which we were now walking. Looking along to the left, the canal is framed by a long scattering of illuminated windows piercing the night, as yet another line of tenements run off at a right angle to us. It is a brilliant view, a side of Edinburgh that obviously never makes the tourist brochures, but which tells its own stories. If you are looking for firm Hearts territory in Edinburgh, then walking over the Union Canal is akin to crossing the Rubicon. We pass a couple of pubs on the left – The Golden Rule, and the Polworth Tavern, both of which are 'Hearts pubs' according to Ross; places he sometimes goes for a pre-match pint. Hibernian supporters obviously associate them with Hearts too, as there was an infamous attack here by the notorious Hibernian casuals a few years back.

This was the beating heart of Scotland's and, for a period, the British Empire's brewing industry. Almost every Edinburgher with working-class roots in the city will have some sort of connection with a brewery via a relative or grandparent who worked in one. And while Edinburgh's breweries were not confined solely to the Gorgie/Dalry neighbourhood of the city, the Union Canal corridor is where the industry was most heavily concentrated, giving the area a very distinctive look and feel.

'It's not so much here that you feel the buzz,' Ross says. 'It's once you cross Dundee Street, and start heading down to the crossroads at Ardmillan, that's where the crowd starts to swell,' although, as he talks, we pass another much more definite 'Hearts pub' as we approach the crossroads, The Diggers (officially the Gravediggers Arms, so named as it sits opposite a cemetery). The junction is fairly quiet, the odd car going past, followed by a double-decker bus, with its two rows of brightly lit but empty seats. Despite the deserted feel, it is not hard to imagine there being a matchday buzz here, as Ross suggests. This is where four of the main routes to Tynecastle converge on to Gorgie Road, like tributaries flowing into the main river. Packed with people buzzing with anticipation, it is easy to see what Ross means, even on this quiet Tuesday evening in February, the air cold and damp and the streets deadened by coronavirus restrictions. We turn left and start walking towards the stadium, along Gorgie Road. Depending on the direction from which you approach, it's not always apparent where Tynecastle actually is, as it's shielded from the main road by high tenements. In fact, if you didn't know better, you certainly wouldn't think there was room to put a stadium there. On visiting Tynecastle for the first time since its redevelopment, a famous Scottish football groundhopper, the Fitbal Nomad, wrote:

My first thought is how have they fitted an almost 20,000-seater stadium into such a small space with old sandstone buildings mere yards away from the back of one stand ... I enter [the] place and gasp. Inside Tynecastle Park is totally changed since my last visit (pre-redevelopment) and utterly gorgeous. Four matching, single tier stands are tight to the pitch and rise steep and high above it. Nowhere in this ground can possibly have a poor view ... I wasn't a huge fan however of the Eiger-like trek up to my seat, but boy the view was worth it.

It is exactly the constraints of the site that give Tynecastle its quite distinctive look and style since its redevelopment. The lack of room at the back of the stadium meant that the supports for the new stands are built into four tall pylons at the front of the stands; one at each corner of the pitch. It is from here that roofs of the new stands are suspended, unlike most modern stadiums which are built as cantilever stands, with the strength coming from the back and holding up the roof from above. This has created problems for Hearts – for example, they have had difficulty in making their pitch bigger due to the pylons (the pitch at Tynecastle is one of the smallest in Scotland) and players regularly lean over into the spectators to retrieve the ball, or lean back against the stand to try and create enough run-up space to take a throw or a corner. This has led to flashpoints over the years where players have come into contact with the fans (both home and away supporters). As you might expect, these have often happened in derby matches, although not exclusively, with players grabbed and punched by fans. The unique aspects of Tynecastle definitely seem to help Hearts, and their home form is usually the bedrock of their season, its small dimensions allowing them to quickly get on top of opponents, starving them of room and time to play.

* * *

Neil and Paul are old school friends, both born and bred in Edinburgh. I meet them in Morningside, one of Edinburgh's villages that is often used as an example of the stuffy side of the city, full of pearl-clutching old women who speak with an exaggeratedly posh Edinburgh accent. It's probably partly true, or at least has been in the past, although it is also now quite a young and trendy area, with lots of students and young professionals, which gives it a vibrancy. The area sits in the south-west of the city centre and, like much of Edinburgh, is characterised by tall and elegant tenement flats that line the main streets, broken periodically by large, beautiful and expensive houses, many of which could be called mansions. It is as middle class an area as you could imagine, and it is absolutely not associated with football. But it does have some nice bars and is handy for the three of us to meet.

Neil was brought up not far from Morningside, in Blackford, also a nice suburban area and it is here he is staying with his mum and dad on this visit home to Edinburgh. Neil moved to Shetland – the islands situated off the north coast of Scotland – where his wife is from. And such is his love of football that after a juvenile career that saw him play for the renowned Hutchison Vale Boys Club (one of Scotland's most successful juvenile clubs that has produced numerous Scottish internationals), he is now the manager of the Shetland Islands' 'national' team. This team represents the archipelago in the International Island Games as well as the annual grudge match against neighbouring islands Orkney. Neil is rightly proud of the fact that he managed his Shetland team to a record 8-0 victory over their great northern rivals Orkney in 2022 – a momentous result for their team, and their community. And while Neil has made his life and is raising his family in Shetland, and while he no doubt enjoyed that victory in Orkney, it is the Edinburgh Derby that is the only match that really gets him excited and nervous beforehand.

'I think Hearts are undoubtedly the third-biggest club in Scotland, bigger and more successful than Hibernian, and also Aberdeen,' he tells me with an earnest certainty. 'They are the dominant team in Edinburgh, the bigger and more successful of the two, a success and an identity that has been built over the decades and is passed on from father to son. They are Edinburgh's team.'[23]

When I ask him why he thinks that might be the case, he explains how he thinks Hibernian have always been a bit of a lower-class team, their support being concentrated in the less affluent areas while Hearts draw their support from all across the city, including the nicer parts and the towns outside Edinburgh. But when I ask if this is a roundabout way of saying that Hearts are the establishment team, he says no, 'I've never understood what that term means, although I have to admit I use it myself, but in an ironic way or if I'm having a joke or winding someone up.'

Paul is also a Hearts fan, but he was brought up in Gorgie, Hearts' home district. He thinks both Hearts and Hibernian have a pretty similar support base, but that Hearts have more fans who attend games because they have been more successful, and he agrees that Hearts are very much 'Edinburgh's team'.

'Think about the name, the Heart of Midlothian, it doesn't get any more Edinburgh than that – it's literally at the centre of the city. I think as well that the whole McCrae's thing might have had an impact, people were different and things like that – the whole king and country thing – mattered to people then.'

It still matters to Hearts. 'The whole McCrae's thing' refers to McCrae's Battalion, the nickname of the 16th Royal Scots during World War One. They were one of the local battalions formed, drawn from specific local communities and as such they were sometimes called 'pals battalions' – which I'm sure made them more appealing at the time, but adds a real poignancy now, knowing what they were about to face. The importance of this story from the club's past is a recurring theme – it is simply impossible to read more than a sentence or two about the history of Hearts without it coming up. So much so in fact that a casual observer could be forgiven for thinking it's one of those modern marketing tropes that clubs pick up on and flog to death. And there are certainly plenty of Hibernian supporters who feel that the whole thing has been abused, particularly in recent years, as a way of petty point scoring, or even trying to reinforce Hearts' credentials as the 'establishment club'. But it doesn't take much investigation to realise the part that this sad but proud episode played in Hearts' history and their identity is huge, and that is absolutely not a modern fabrication or embellishment; on the contrary, it is almost impossible to appreciate through cynical 21st-century eyes what it must have meant and so, if anything, its significance is probably underplayed.

More than 35,000 people crowded around Haymarket in Edinburgh, a busy road junction at the west end of town, to mark the unveiling of the war memorial, a tribute to those Hearts players and supporters who lost their lives in World War One.

A tall pylon with clocks by James Ritchie & Son embedded in its yellow stone edifice, Harry Gamley's design chiselled the names of various engagements into the sides: Vimy, Ypres, Gaza, Somme. A plaque on the front reads 'Erected by the Heart of Midlothian Football Club to the memory of their players and members who fell in the Great War 1914–1919'.[24]

It must have been a sombre occasion; the loss and sacrifice that every family in Scotland experienced would have still felt recent to everyone there: 'There were many wreaths laid at the bottom of the memorial that day, including tributes from the League, Hearts players, and other clubs including Celtic, Leith Athletic, and Portsmouth.' I don't need to point out whose name is not mentioned among the 'other clubs', although it is mentioned in a different Hearts account of that era, as one of the 75 clubs from whom players enlisted. Another memorial, and the battalions' colours were handed over to St Giles Cathedral in Edinburgh for safekeeping, and they now rest in the same corner as a memorial to John Knox.[25]

In the December of 1914 Hearts issued a rallying call before a derby match with Hibernian offering free entrance to any volunteers, with the instruction that 'Sir George McCrae will be glad if you will "fall in" at the foot of Ardmillan Terrace [a junction just along from Tynecastle Park where many roads converge on to Gorgie Road].' 'Hibernian was one of the clubs whose players had to that point mostly sat tight instead of joining ... But before the Hearts–Hibs derby on December 5th, word began to circulate that Hibs' star defender Sandy Grosert had joined McCrae's.'[26] When the regiment would later parade though the centre of town, the crowd shouted 'good old Hearts' as members of the team were recognised. A poem published in the *Dundee People's Journal* on 13 March 2015 captured the spirit of the time:

> When the Empire is in danger, and we hear our country's call,
>
> The Motherland may count on us to leave the leather ball.

We've hacked our way in many a fray, we've
passed and gone for goal,

But a bigger field awaits us, and we're keen to
join the roll.

So it's right wing, left wing, front line, and goal;

Half back and full back, every living soul;

Sound o' wind, storn o' limb, eager for the fray,

Every soul for the goal –

'Hearts!' 'Hearts!' 'Hearts,' lead the way![27]

The push from Hearts had come after some stinging letters
started appearing in the media calling into question the
morality of footballers who were staying at home:

> The principal target of this vitriol was the
> Edinburgh team, Heart of Midlothian – then
> leaders of the Scottish League and considered by
> contemporary observers to be the finest football
> combination in Great Britain ... A letter to
> the press, renaming the club 'White Feathers
> of Midlothian', presaged a stream of angry and
> insulting missives. Many included detailed
> directions to the nearest recruiting office.

Hearts' establishment credentials also mean they have
a long connection to the British military dating back to
1914 and the outbreak of World War One. So much so in
fact that Heart of Midlothian are officially the football
team of the Royal Navy's new aircraft carrier, HMS

Queen Elizabeth, which was built at Rosyth dockyard, near Edinburgh.

Why were Hearts targeted more than other clubs? At least part of Hearts' confidence in their position as Edinburgh's 'premier club' comes from their place as the club of the Edinburgh establishment, the middle class, respectable club of Edinburgh. Historically, in Scotland and in particular Edinburgh, being part of the establishment was synonymous with being Protestant; Edinburgh as the capital city is the home of the Church of Scotland and was where the reformation started under the preacher John Knox. Albert Mackie's history of Hearts (published in 1959) is an amazing window into the period, a period before books about football, and football clubs. The language is of its time, but it is all the richer for it.

It is striking how the book immediately talks, not about Hearts supporters, but about Edinburghers, and uses 'our club' and other such descriptions easily (Mackie himself wrote for the Edinburgh newspaper the *Edinburgh Evening News*, the proprietor of which had been part of the business consortium who had taken ownership of the new plc after they folded the old version of the club in 1906). I do not for a moment think Mackie was some very early version of an internet troll, and so we have to assume that such language was normal; that the inference that Edinburghers and Hearts supporters are one and the same was an uncontroversial opinion, perfectly in keeping with the learned and conversational style of the book. Indeed, Mackie tries to address this very point on the first page:

I do not believe any other football club in the world can lay claim to have aroused and retained such warmth of affection, and this from a people (meaning Edinburghers) who do not make a practice of displaying their emotions. Edinburgh is the home to a rival First Division club, Hibernian, but it is no disparagement of Hibs to state that it is Hearts who hold the devotion of the city as a whole.

Mackie goes on to allude to historical reasons for this favouritism. Given that Mackie was writing in the late 50s, just after Hibernian had won three championships in five years (in contrast to Hearts' own trophy hoodoo of 50 years, which Mackie described as a well-known Scottish music hall joke), he can't have been referring to on-field fortunes, or at least not solely. So what exactly are the historical reasons that Hearts saw themselves as Edinburgh's club?

Perhaps chief among them is the sacrifice made by Hearts players in joining up with McCrae's Battalion. Not that it should matter when talking about such a brave step, but the fact that this was a promising Hearts team who had started the new season in great form, does add a sense of *'what if'*, helping to magnify the sense of World War One as a waste of so much young promise; a sense that is of course not limited to Hearts, or even to football.

It is difficult now to understand the sense of duty and British patriotism that existed around the war. Britain was still a major imperial force in the world, using its military (and those of her imperial subjects) to conquer, rule and exploit the resources of huge swathes of the globe, all backed by the ever-powerful Royal Navy. Even in Scotland, which in those days had not really begun on its journey to reimagining itself as a nation in its own right, at least not in any organised way, that sense of proud Britishness, so absent in Scotland today, was a powerful force. And Edinburgh, being the city of the establishment in Scotland, would no doubt have been keener than most to burnish its 'good citizens' credentials by showing up well in defence of king and country.

Given this context, it is not hard to see how this conspicuous sacrifice by a football team would attract so much admiration and respect from the good people of Edinburgh. In fact, looking back it is hard to imagine a better way for a football club to position itself as the team of respectable Edinburgh, as 'our team', than by leading the way that the rest of the city could follow. It was football club meets civic pride, all mixed together with a very tangible sense of sacrifice, honour and patriotism. It is easy to see why the city should have taken them to their hearts, and for them to have become 'Edina's Darlings'. As Aiden Smith, a journalist with *The Scotsman*, put in his book *Heartfelt*:

> Hearts fans would maintain that they are *the* Edinburgh, Edinburgh's *only* club. 'Come on, the Edinburgh team!' is a cry heard at Tynecastle, asserting Hearts' status as the capital outfit, the establishment team, who stand ramrod-straight

on the ramparts of Edinburgh Castle and scoff and sneer at the serfs using the boar's head for a football down in Leith ... So where does this idea of superiority come from? Well, Hearts, as I say, are the establishment club. I know a lot of policemen who are Hearts fans. I have a hunch a lot of bank managers are Hearts fans.

Smith is a Hibernian supporter and was writing in a book about his switching allegiances to follow Hearts for a season, and so there is more than a touch of the melodramatic about his descriptions, but nonetheless it helps to illustrate the perception that exists. There was always a sense among Hibernian supporters that Hearts were treated preferentially by the Edinburgh Council, and indeed many prominent councillors and politicians have made no secret of their links to Hearts. And they have always gone out of their way to maintain links to the aristocracy, and their patron even to this day is the Earl of Rosebery; Hearts even recently had an away strip (in slightly garish yellow and pink hoops) in the Rosebery colours as a tribute to that family. Hearts are proud of such establishment links, and indeed try to play them up. Hibernian fans would scoff at the obsequiousness of it all, how Hearts fans are the punctilious social climbers, striving always to attract the attention of, and get a pat on the head from, their betters while they obediently doff their caps out of a deeply ingrained sense of duty and respect for authority. Could that be a throwback to the McCrae's days, that need for approval from their betters, the unquestioning acceptance that what someone with a title says must be right?

* * *

One of Edinburgh's main concert halls, The Usher Hall, is a grand-looking venue that is set back slightly from the incessant traffic of Lothian Road in the city centre. In keeping with Edinburgh's history, it was built by the Usher family using the enormous fortune they made from brewing, to give something back to their home city (as is McEwan Hall, another of the city's concert halls built by the eponymous brewing giant). It is a semi-circular building with entrances around the outside, and tucked at one corner at its northern side is a large flagstone on the ground commemorating the place where a 'grand recruitment meeting' was held on 27 November 1914, to enlist men to join McCrae's own battalion. The commemorative stone ends with large capital letters stating that:

Edinburgh remembers them with pride

It's hard not to notice that this line is almost identical to the last line in the chorus of the Hearts song:

Auld Reekie supports them with pride [28]

CHAPTER 9

INTER-WAR YEARS

1919–1938

WHEN HEARTS took the field against St Mirren in the Victory Cup Final in 1919, it seemed like a small measure of natural justice was to come their way. Hearts had become associated more than most with the loss of a generation of young men in the Great War. While winning a football trophy would have been scant consolation for those killed and maimed, it would have been a fitting tribute to the role played by their football club. But we all know how horribly unsentimental the fates of football can be.

There were 60,000 at Celtic Park to see a tight final, and after a 0-0 draw at the end of normal time, the match went to extra time. It was here that Hearts' dream ended, as the roof caved in and St Mirren scored three quick goals to take the final and the cup by 3-0. There was a neat historical tie-in that Hearts' losing manager, John McCartney, was the father of the man who would lead Hibernian to defeat in the final of the Victory Cup after World War Two, Willie McCartney.

While lost silverware is always jarring, and while it would have been a fitting tribute to the never-to-be-fulfilled talents of that lost Hearts team, the aftermath of the Great War was about survival for both clubs. While both had scraped through, they certainly had not emerged unscathed and their finances were in poor shape. The Victory Cup helped by injecting some much-needed gate money into both clubs because, as well as Hearts reaching the final, Hibernian managed, via a series of home draws (which were badly needed for income), to reach the semi-final before losing 3-0 to St Mirren, the Paisley club completing an Edinburgh double by winning the trophy. Just as the clubs were starting to look to the future, the Spanish flu epidemic ripped through Scotland, as if people hadn't suffered enough already. For Hibernian it inflicted upon them a grievous loss.

Dan McMichael, their manager and general club stalwart, succumbed to the pandemic. One of the driving forces behind the survival and revival of the club in the early 1890s, McMichael was a towering figure and a huge loss for a club that was already struggling at the lower end of the league. In fact, Hibernian's form was so poor in this era that the best they would do in the coming years was a solitary third-place finish in 1925, which came on the back of two consecutive Scottish Cup Final appearances in 1923 and 1924 (both lost, to Celtic and Airdrieonians respectively). Otherwise it was a slog, and Hibernian would hover around the bottom of the division until eventually succumbing to what must have seemed like an inevitable relegation in 1931.

For Hearts the early 1920s were also a struggle and, apart from a single third place in 1921, they jumped between struggling at the bottom of the league to mid-table mediocrity. The toll of the war, not to mention the financial struggles that preceded it, were taking time to get over. But by the mid-1920s Hearts finished third again, kick-starting an upturn in their fortunes that would slowly build in the 1930s. By the start of that decade Hearts were once more a fixture near the top of the league, finishing third twice, fourth once and second in 1937/38.

Hearts' pre-war identity was as a club everyone liked and respected, who were a nice club but not a winning club. The thousands of people who turned out at the unveiling of the Hearts war memorial in 1922 show how much Hearts' story during the war resonated with the wider Edinburgh public, and even to the wider Scottish public. It is easy to pour scorn on this sense of patriotism and sacrifice looking back now – and indeed Hibernian fans will make pointed comments about how Hearts 'single-handedly won World War One for king and country' as a way to sarcastically minimise it, but it is clear from the contemporary accounts that this was a really big deal. The fact it still plays such a central story in Hearts' identity to this day shows just how important it was to them as a club. While they didn't win any major honours, it does seem to be where their Edina's Darlings identity was cemented off the pitch, and perhaps on the pitch as well.

As the Great War was raging, the Easter Rising in Dublin in 1916 kicked off the sequence of events that would lead to Irish independence from Great Britain, and also the partition of Ireland. The fledgling Irish Free State then spent some years in a kind of national limbo, mostly but not completely free of British rule, trying to find a way to build a modern nation state while wrestling with a huge number of structural problems. This may seem incidental to Hibernian and the Edinburgh Derby, but it mattered. Hibernian were still wholly owned by Irish families, and it seems entirely reasonable that their attention and resources might have been elsewhere during these years of war in their homeland. Indeed, it's a question that football historian Andy Mitchell raised with me – just how much was it coincidence that the worst period in Hibernian's history on the field coincided with these events off the field? It's certainly safe to assume that many at Hibernian felt they needed new blood to freshen up the *ould Irish* who had hitherto owned and run the club. The problem in the past had been there were no 'respectable' Edinburgh businessmen interested in investing in the Irish club. That was until Harry Swan came along.

On the pitch, Hibernian – in hindsight, very naively – were still trying to reclaim their crown as the premier Irish club in Scotland from Celtic. The 1923 Scottish Cup Final was that moment and, as if to show the strong bonds that still inked the two clubs, the opposing managers were brothers, Alec and Willie Maley (Willie Maley and his other brother Tom had both played for Hibernian) and Hibs' star forward was an ex-Celtic player, Jimmy McColl. The familial bonds, and the collective singing of Irish songs by the crowd, wasn't enough, and Celtic won the final.

In Scottish football terms, the 1920s and 30s is the first period of what we would all now recognise, but back then was just beginning: Old Firm dominance. They had always been strong and competitive, but never before had they strangled all the other clubs to the same extent. Since the now-defunct Third Lanark (another Glasgow team) won the title in 1903/04, Celtic and Rangers shared the championship between them for all but one year until the outbreak of World War Two (Motherwell in 1931/32) – 35 seasons and 34 Old Firm title wins. It puts what we are living through now into a depressing historical context, and also serves only to make the post-war era all the more remarkable. With regards the Edinburgh Derby, it's an interesting time, as in many ways it is this era that set the narrative that still exists today. Looking back with contemporary eyes on this period is difficult; Dundee United were only just changing their name from Dundee Hibernian and hadn't yet troubled the upper levels of Scottish football; Aberdeen had also not really risen to prominence, and for Hibernian it was the worst period in their history. This meant that Hearts could genuinely lay claim to being the third force in Scotland, and undoubtedly the top dogs in Edinburgh, where they hammered home their advantage over the flailing Hibs.

And yet for Hearts, it was a period that got away from them, a time when they should have pressed home their advantages and nailed their place as the undoubted third force in Scottish football; as we have seen so often with the Edinburgh clubs, it was an opportunity that they didn't make the most of, and Hearts would end this period not as the natural challenger to the Old Firm, but as a music-hall joke for their lack of success.

The Scottish Cup was still a bit more open to the other clubs, although it didn't help Hearts. Third Lanark, Dundee, Falkirk, Partick Thistle, Greenock Morton, Airdrieonians, St Mirren, Kilmarnock, East Fife and Clyde all won it; and while Hibernian made three finals in the period, Hearts never made it past the semi-finals despite four attempts; it's easy to see why Hearts' cup record had become such an object of mirth around Scottish football.

Of course nobody knew the war was going to come, and that it would be so utterly devastating when it did, to the point where it acted as a restart. Society changed completely, the UK's politics changed, and Scottish football changed. For the second time – although less tragically this time – Hearts' progress in slowly building a strong team again through the 1930s was interrupted by European great power politics. And just as the storm clouds of fascism were building over continental Europe, Edinburgh was having its own flirtation with extreme politics that must have had an impact on the way that its good citizens viewed their football clubs.

CHAPTER 10

RELIGION

'CAPITAL DUO in blast at UEFA' screamed the headline on the back of the *Edinburgh Evening News*.[29]

'Edinburgh's Big Two today joined forces to blast UEFA after they branded Hibs and Hearts as sectarian outfits,' the story continued. It went on to describe how the UEFA website had written about the two clubs in a profile section. Hibernian 'have come to represent the Catholic community in the Scottish capital', while Hearts were described as a 'badge of honour for the Scottish capital's Protestant community'. A Hibernian official distanced themselves, calling the descriptions archaic, out of touch, regrettable and inaccurate. The Hearts official urged UEFA to 'drag themselves into the 21st century', calling the description 'absolutely shocking'. The very next day the *Edinburgh Evening News* ran with the headline '*UEFA forced to back down*', after they agreed to delete the offending copy from their website.

Both clubs were annoyed at these descriptions – they were reductive and fell into the trap of seeing everything through the lens of the Old Firm. But then again, UEFA didn't just make this stuff up, did they? Where did they get the idea from in the first place?

Religion is a touchy subject for Edinburgh football, as it often is for wider Scottish society. It is often the elephant in the room, or the slightly inappropriate old uncle that both sides have made a silent pact to ignore and to keep away from family parties. It is an aspect of Edinburgh society, and in turn Edinburgh football, that people are uncomfortable with. And it just doesn't suit the taciturn Edinburgh demeanour to talk about such things openly. To this day people will say that you shouldn't talk about politics or religion as it doesn't lead to anything good; UEFA obviously didn't get that memo.

Any mention of religion usually provokes in Hearts and Hibernian supporters a reaction that is strong and reflexive, even angry, before the very idea is quickly dismissed as 'nothing to do with football', or a 'leave that shite to the Old Firm'. And yet, when researching this book it is a subject that popped up again and again, often unprompted, and usually quite near the start of a conversation. It is usually in the context of why it is irrelevant to the conversation, or why it shouldn't be mentioned. But then I kept finding myself wondering, why bring it up at all? It's a point that academic researchers from the University of Edinburgh, Kelly & Bairner, also encountered as they conducted research for a 2018 paper on the subject: 'A significant feature of a high number of interviews conducted with fans … was the determination shown by Hibs and Hearts supporters to emphasise that they are not sectarian. This was often evident in the respondents' body language and facial responses when they appeared uncomfortable, suspicious and even defensive when first introducing (or being introduced to) questions relating to religious and Irish issues.'

In a book interviewing Hibernian supporters – *We are Hibernian*[30] – on what the club means to them, every single person mentioned religion and its role in their support of Hibernian – even if it was to say it had no bearing. These people were either volunteering this information, which would be odd for something of no relevance, or the interviewer was asking them, which would also be odd if it had no bearing. And so the obvious question is, why does this thing that supposedly has nothing to do with football in Edinburgh keep coming up in relation to football in Edinburgh?

And then I noticed something. Neither Hibernian nor Hearts denied UEFA's statement; they both talked about being 'out of touch', 'archaic' and that UEFA should 'get into the 21st century'. So do these rebuttals actually mean these descriptions were once true, but not true anymore? And, if so, when did they cease to be true? Who decided, and what, if any, lasting effect did it have on the Edinburgh rivalry?

* * *

Firstly it is worth stating upfront that most Hibs and Hearts fan today are not religious, and religion plays little (if any at all) part in their support for their clubs. Most Hearts and Hibernian fans bristle at the suggestion, because to make the association is to align their clubs with the Old Firm, something they hate to do. And for the most part, they are right; the Edinburgh rivalry is not a mini-Old Firm match, and the history of both clubs and of the Old Firm are very different. It is a lazy assumption, and one that – like much in Scottish football – is only possible when everything is viewed through an Old Firm lens (which applies to the vast majority of the Scottish fitba media). For all manner of reasons, not least the very different histories of Edinburgh and Glasgow, it is inaccurate. However, saying that the Edinburgh Derby has little to do with the Old Firm is not the same as saying that it has little to do with religion. In fact, excluding the Old Firm from the equation, it could be reasonably argued that the Edinburgh Derby has a greater religious subtext and backstory than almost any other fixture in the UK and maybe even in Europe.

As the capital, Edinburgh has been at the heart of much of the intrigue, history, wars and conquest that has dominated the history of Scotland. Since the reformations in Scotland and England, religion has been central to much of that history, from Mary Queen of Scots to the Jacobites. The English Reformation basically took the Roman Church and adapted it slightly so that it answered to London instead of Rome but kept many of its practices and rituals. As a result, the Anglican Church – known as the Episcopalian Church in Scotland – looks and sounds a lot like its Roman Catholic predecessor. The Scottish Reformation took on a more extreme form and instead embraced the pious austerity of Calvinism/Presbyterianism, a style that fits (and is possibly responsible for) Edinburgh's reputation as reserved, stuffy, undemonstrative, even a bit dull.

The more extreme Scottish Reformation resulted in the creation of the Church of Scotland, Presbyterian, and fiercely independent. It is a testament to this independence that, as the Scottish nobility were selling out Scottish independence to England in 1707, the Church of Scotland was protected from being absorbed into the Anglican Church. This meant that as Scotland was absorbed into the UK and shorn of the institutions of statehood, and its governance was moved to London, the power of the Church was made greater in Scotland. In fact for centuries the closest thing Scotland had to a parliament was the General Assembly of the Church of Scotland, the annual meeting of the Church held in its imposing building above The Mound in Edinburgh where it decided its – and by extension Scotland's – rules.[31] As a result, it held a central place within the city's life. 'Nothing, not even the vindication of national independence a quarter of a millennium before [referring to the 13th and 14th century Scottish Wars of Independence] has so marked Edinburgh's character.'

This is where the comparisons with the Old Firm don't work. Glasgow's population boomed with the industrial revolution, and so the Irish Catholic immigrants were part of its growth and helped to shape its character to a far greater extent than they ever did in Edinburgh. Also, Irish immigration to Glasgow brought with it high numbers of Protestant Ulster Irish, who brought with them their own particular brand of religion, something that never happened in Edinburgh, where the Catholic population was small and contained in a specific, often separate, community, which created a very different dynamic than in Glasgow.

> The isolation and weakness of the Irish in Edinburgh meant that they were despised, rather than actively feared or resented ... but prejudice towards them was endemic and it helped to keep them together ... In the Cowgate and Leith, they congregated out of a feeling of kinship and for protection, as strangers in a strange land.

Is it then possible that Edinburgh football, unlike almost any other institution in Edinburgh at the time, managed to exist in a religious vacuum? Well, we already know that Hibernian were proudly, overtly and officially a religious club for the first half of their existence. We also know that John Hope, father of football in Edinburgh and founder of the 3rd ERV Football Club who won the first ever Edinburgh FA Cup, was fiercely anti-Catholic, and ensured that his 3rd ERV club was for Protestants only. One prominent academic, Professor Gerry Finn, who studies religion in Scotland, wrote:

> It can be no surprise that the character of the 3rd ERV was Protestant ... Indeed, the necessity of maintaining the Protestant nature of political and civil life was a common argument

advanced by [John] Hope. Any organisations or institutions that included Catholics had no place in Parliament, questioned their presence in the Edinburgh police force, and implied that they had no legitimate role anywhere within the power of the British State.[32]

Any institution, even the Edinburgh Football Association? Hibernian FC were refused entry to both the Edinburgh and Scottish FAs on account of them being an Irish Catholic club, and not a 'Scottish' club. It's suggested that the power Hope wielded within the association through his 3rd ERV club was one of the main reasons for this local hostility.[33] The blanket ban imposed by the Edinburgh FA on any of their member clubs even playing against Hibernian was actually ignored by Hearts at the risk of censure, hence the first match taking place that Christmas Day in 1875. Writing in 1924, Reid's official history of Hearts noted:

> Interest in the game in Edinburgh was really created by the old-time meetings of the Hearts and the Hibernians, into which there then entered racial jealousy, even sectarian bitterness.

He goes on to suggest this manifested itself early on:

> It is on record that on the occasion of one of the first meetings of the clubs in the Scottish Cup competition the Hearts players went to Easter

Road stripped for the fray and neither entered the pavilion of their opponents before nor after the match.[34]

Bringing our perspective back to the 21st century, the same day of the UEFA sectarianism scandal headline on the back page of the *Edinburgh Evening News*, there was another story in the sidebar, the headline of which was 'Tynecastle Security Move Pays Dividend'. This story quotes the same Hearts official who had described the UEFA description as 'absolutely shocking', hailing the success of the extra security measures that had been put in place for the previous weekend's visit of Celtic to Tynecastle. 'Given tensions between the two sets of supporters at past Tynecastle encounters, Hearts increased their police and stewarding presence', resulting in a 50 per cent drop in arrests since the last match between the two clubs at Tynecastle. The news story then explained what some of these tensions were:

> The dual problem of racism and sectarianism had still been evident at the match. The game … was accompanied by the standard sectarian chanting coming from both sets of fans, but the abuse meted out to Celtic's Bobo Baldé [a black player] from a small but vocal section of the home support was disturbing. The 'monkey chants' directed at the defender [Baldé] were especially disappointing.

A profile of the club (presumably written by a foreigner with a passing knowledge of Edinburgh and Scottish football) was described as 'absolutely shocking' for labelling Hearts as 'the Protestant club', while on the very same back page, the same club official hails the success of the additional security measures he had to put in place, because it meant only half as many arrests as they had in the previous game for racist and sectarian behaviour by supporters when playing Celtic. There is a certain irony there, which I'm sure the UEFA official whose work was attacked so strenuously would have enjoyed.

Of course, we need to acknowledge that there is a difference between what a club officially says and does, and what its support (or sections of its support) say and do. The two things are regularly different, and even discussing a support as if it is some hive mind is misleading. There are factions and extremes within supports. In many ways these extremes are caricatures of the wider support, but they are also often the main factor in shaping the perceptions of others as to the true nature of a support.

We all do it. Do we really believe that all Millwall fans are shaven-headed far-right hooligans? No, and yet we would casually characterise Millwall as a far-right club. Likewise Celtic supporters as left-wing IRA supporters, Tottenham Hotspur as the 'Jewish club' in London, Barcelona as Spain-hating Catalan nationalists, Lazio as far-right, Livorno as left-wing, Sevilla as rich, Real Betis as poor.

These identities can be both true in a very superficial way, while at the same time not true in a very official way.

I doubt any of these clubs go out of the way to endorse or promote the views of their more extreme supporters (although I'm sure many will turn a blind eye), and I'm sure the views don't represent the entire support. So when Hibs and Hearts describe their characterisation as Catholic and Protestant as archaic, they are right. But archaic doesn't mean untrue, it means old-fashioned or out-of-date – which suggests that it was at least once true. So, when was it true, when did it stop being true, and what residual influence has it left on the derby?

* * *

One of Edinburgh's most famous districts is Morningside. It is an upper-middle-class area, made up mostly of elaborate tenements and grand townhouses, all bisected by a long main road – Morningside Road – that runs out from the city centre towards the suburbs of the Braid Hills and, eventually, the Pentland Hills to the south. It is a highly desirable area to live in and, as such, it is very expensive. It also long had a reputation for being the part of Edinburgh that you were most likely to find the classic, snooty Edinburgh woman with her airs and graces and anglified accent. It is not an area particularly associated with football, but at the top of Morningside Road there is a busy junction, which has become known as Holy Corner.

Holy Corner is so-called because at each of the four corners of the junction stands a church; and there is a fifth just up the road. Amazingly, all five were from different branches of the Christian faith (Episcopalian, Baptist,

Church of Scotland, Congregationalist and Free Church of Scotland). Holy Corner perfectly encapsulates how important – and popular – religion was in Edinburgh, but also how alien the Roman Catholic faith was to Edinburgh that it is not represented at Holy Corner. The churches are not still all in business, although three of them are, but the buildings remain, in what is a nice metaphor for religion in Edinburgh; it is not as popular or important as it once was, but it remains part of the very fabric of the city and its character.

In Scotland, we have separate schooling for Catholics. This is a divisive issue for many reasons, but it has been the case since 1918. However, only Roman Catholic schools designate themselves as religious schools. Normal schools are just normal schools, not overtly religious. Yet when I attended Bruntsfield Primary School not far from Holy Corner in the 1980s (a 'normal' school), we used to have 'hymn practice' every Tuesday, and what was called 'service' every Thursday (basically an assembly), where we would sing the hymns we had practised and get a sermon from the local Church of Scotland minister, as well as the usual assembly stuff. I can distinctly remember that Reverend Gordon's sermon was once based on Hearts' famous win (probably their most famous European result ever) when they beat Bayern Munich 1-0 at Tynecastle in the UEFA Cup. Tying football and religion together that way always stuck in my mind, although the exact details of the sermon are now fuzzy (something about how one man – Ian Ferguson, the scorer of the Hearts goal – could lead thousands in celebration and joy). I never really understood the difference between Catholics and Protestants, and the hymn service had always been there, so was just normal; it never even dawned on my young mind that it was religious. Although I do remember wondering why my Scots–Asian classmates would stay in the classrooms and not join in, but that was also just normal. And at Bruntsfield Primary, normal meant Church of Scotland Presbyterianism; and why wouldn't it? This was Edinburgh, and the established church, the established religion was Church of Scotland Presbyterianism. Was the same true of Hearts? Were they the 'Protestant team' simply because they were the normal team, the Edinburgh team, the established, and establishment, team? And because the Catholics had a club, it was only right that there was a club for the 'normal' Scots?

In 1884, the *Scottish Athletic Journal* wrote:

'In response to a defeat by Hibernian, there was talk that Hearts were considering becoming an explicitly anti-Catholic club, by creating a "team of Orangemen" to act as a cultural and sporting counterweight to Hibernian.'

This is exactly what happened in Glasgow, when Rangers, who at the start of their history had not been explicitly anti-Catholic, did take up the call and become the 'team of Orangemen' to take on Celtic, thanks in part to the influence of Protestant Ulster shipyard workers moving to Rangers' home patch in Govan.

It's to the credit of Hearts that they never did take this direction, but the very fact it was ever considered does suggest that there was something in the Edinburgh

Derby – even as early as the 1880s – to do with religious antagonisms and motivations, as much as the football challenges. Does this explain why Hearts, and not one of the multitude of other Edinburgh clubs around at that time, emerged as the main challenger to Hibernian in these early years?

It is something that Andy Mitchell, the historian of Edinburgh football, also mentioned – that while there were many reasons that Hearts emerged as one of the top clubs from early Edinburgh football, the religious aspect was one of them. And while Hearts may not have explicitly embraced Orangeism in those early days, they didn't have to. Orangeism was not an Edinburgh thing, it was an Ulster (and, by extension, Glasgow) thing. Hearts didn't need to become explicitly Protestant, because as Edinburgh's club they already were – it was implicit to their identity as Edina's Darlings, just as Bruntsfield Primary didn't need to be a Protestant school. The less overt role of religion in the shaping of the derby fits with the traditional reserved character of Edinburgh. As Isobel Mackay put it in her husband's authorised biography, 'David came from a lovely, lovely family. His parents, brothers. All his aunts and uncles. But we never spoke about Hearts and Hibs as my family were all Hibs. Another thing was I was Catholic and David was Protestant. Religion was never really spoken about. We got round it.' In Mackie's history of Hearts, he makes numerous references to this stoney, perhaps even cold, exterior for which Edinburgh and her people were famed. Things were seldom overt or demonstrative, it just wasn't the done thing, *it just wasn't spoken about.*

When you consider the social and historical context, the fact that religion and religious discrimination was a normal part of Scottish and Edinburgh society – indeed, it was an official Church of Scotland policy – it seems impossible that this was not also the case in football; a game which so often serves as a magnifying glass for existing social pressures. When you add in the fact that Hearts were 'Edinburgh's club', and have defined themselves as such from the very early days, it becomes difficult not to see a religious subtext there.

And then another question is why was it with Hibernian – the overtly Catholic and Irish nationalist club – that Hearts struck up their keen rivalry so quickly, where so much *needle* quickly developed? Some of it can undoubtedly be put down to the fact that Hibernian established themselves as one of the top clubs early on, and were starting to dominate. But given the presence of such animosity between the two so early on, it seems impossible that the dominant religious animosity of the time didn't play at least some part.

Protestant extremism is not unknown in Edinburgh; John Cormack, a rabble-rousing bigot, led a fringe political movement called Protestant Action, a group that incredibly won almost 30 per cent of the vote in local elections. Funnily enough their votes were concentrated in the Gorgie and Leith areas of the city. Cormack was following in the line of Edinburgh anti-Catholicism that came from (and was funded by) John Hope, the same man who helped create and establish Edinburgh football back in Victorian times and who was quite possibly involved in the exclusion of Hibernian in those early days. His 3rd ERV territorial army regiment – which was Protestant only – also became the basis of the 16th Royal Scots in World War One – McCrae's Battalion. And while there is no suggestion that religious exclusion was part of McCrae's Battalion, it does further demonstrate the dominant culture of the time and perhaps is why the focus of its recruitment was on Hearts.

The Church of Scotland, as late as the 1920s, was campaigning against Irish immigration, and one member of the Church's subcommittee on the issue remarked that Scots could not be expected to live next to 'weeds' and cautioned against their disloyalty to the UK, and their revolutionary ideas. This was extreme, even for this time, in the Church of Scotland, but it was by no means rare. One former Moderator (the elected leader of the Church), Reverend John White, commented that the Scottish race had to be protected from being 'corrupted by the introduction of a horde of Irish immigrants'. The UK government in London was lobbied by a committee of Presbyterians to stop Irish immigration.

Rev. John White, when reappointed Moderator of the Church in 1930, stated that the newly reunited Church of Scotland (it had just recovered from one of its periodic schisms) would combat Catholicism and the 'menace' of Irish immigration. To its shame, one committee of the Church urged it to join the International League for the

Defence and Furtherance of Protestantism (ILDFP), which was an organisation based in Berlin, dominated by the Nazi Party and, predictably, strongly anti-Semitic and anti-Catholic. Fortunately more moderate voices prevailed and the Church didn't follow up on the recommendation to openly flirt with fascism in the name of combatting Catholicism.[35] Indeed, the language of race, domination and dangerous aliens that was frequent at this time in discussion about Catholicism in Scotland – and which Cormack and his fellow rabble-rousers managed to exploit for electoral success – does take on a more sinister hue when set against the context of what similar attitudes across mainland Europe led to in the 1930s.

As Edinburgh society has moved on, and become dominantly atheist, the football clubs and their supporters have followed suit, and it would be difficult for anyone to argue that religion plays a significant part in either club's identity today. But is it possible, and is it even desirable, for a club to ignore the foundations on which it was built, especially if it left a legacy which still impacts upon the derby?

It is not a coincidence that in the three Scottish cities that host intra-city derbies – Edinburgh, Glasgow and Dundee – the recognised 'establishment' club is the one that stood as opponents to the clubs that represented the immigrant Irish Catholic communities – Hearts, Dundee, Rangers. The coincidence could be extended further, that all of those 'establishment' clubs held the upper hand over their rivals for decades, but that advantage has been eroded and in the case of both Glasgow and Dundee completely overturned in the latter years of the 20th century and into the 21st century, at the same time as society modernised, transparency increased and religion steadily lost its influence.

Now the religious context in Scottish football is complex, as it brings in elements of nationalism (competing nationalisms, in fact) and politics. As a result, being a Protestant club in modern Scotland is associated with British nationalism, most commonly manifested as the waving of the Union flag. This might not seem controversial; after all, it is technically the national flag of Scotland (as part of the UK). But it is a flag with a very specific meaning in Scottish football. It will never be seen at Scotland national team matches, for example, and few, if any, supports will ever be seen flying one. Those that do are invariably those associated with Protestantism/ Unionism; Rangers being the obvious one, but other clubs such as Airdrieonians. There is a small section of Hearts fans who routinely fly that flag, and Hearts have always had a fringe element who were supporters of anti-Catholic, right-wing groups. It's important to emphasise that most Hearts fans view them with disdain and do not want their club associated with it.

The same could be said for Hibernian and the more extreme views of their fans, with their loose Irish nationalism. Pro-IRA chants were fairly common until the 1980s, and Irish flags and symbols are regularly displayed, and while not in and of themselves sectarian or anti-Protestant, they are loaded with Irish Republican connotations in the context of Scottish football; notions that many fans of other clubs (and some of Hibernian themselves) find offensive, or at least unhelpful or anachronistic. Up until the 1950s Hibernian were seen, and were happy to be seen, as the Irish/Catholic club of Edinburgh, and until 1892 Hibernian had a Catholics-only policy, the only club in the history of Scottish football to have such a policy. It was not until the post-war era that Hibernian's uncomfortable sense of itself really began, as it tried to transition away from its heritage, but seemed unsure what it was transitioning to.

One of the most high-profile and overtly religious incidents occurred in 2005, when Hearts fans – and not just a small minority – disrupted the minute's silence held to mark the death of Pope John Paul II. A more overt display of anti-Catholic sentiment would be difficult to find. Kelly & Bairner, the academics who have studied the identities of both Hearts and Hibernian, wrote that:

> This was followed by a mixed reaction among Hearts supporters' spokespeople, with some refusing to condemn the supporters' actions. These incidents led to media attention from around the world and bolstered the perception … of Hearts supporters exhibiting sectarianism. The Hearts supporters are also known for singing 'the Gorgie Boys' with the lyrics 'we're up to our knees in Fenian blood'.

Wallace Mercer, the former Hearts owner and chief executive, also passed comment on the associations that some of the Hearts supporters had:

> When I came to Tynecastle the club had a major social problem, which was partly linked to the lack of performance on the field and partly to bigotry. The first day I joined the club I was invited to join the Masons. My father was a Mason and I wouldn't say anything to criticise that organisation. But I decided at the moment I took over the mantle of responsibility for Hearts that they would be a non-religious, non-political club.

This chapter started with the statements of indignation by both clubs, and on a superficial level those statements were genuine; neither Heart of Midlothian nor Hibernian have given official succour to the more extreme views that exist within their club's supports in our modern era, although it was 1981 when Mercer was invited to join the Masons, presumably by people at Hearts.[36] But football clubs aren't only about the officials with their club ties, and while it is easy to dismiss groups of fans as extreme, it is usually instructive as to which way they lean. Right-wing British nationalists and anti-Catholic agitators don't follow Hibernian because it would be completely at odds with that club's history and identity. Likewise, Irish Republicans don't follow Hearts for the same reasons. And while the extreme voices within their supports may be on the fringe, the truth is they have been part of their clubs for 150 years now. Are there any other derbies in the UK – apart from the obvious exception – that has 150 years of religion and religiously derived cultures and identities as part of its history?

CHAPTER 11

THE POST-WAR BOOM

1946–1965

THE GOLDEN Years: Hibernian in the Days of the Famous Five, and *Hearts: The Golden Years*. There aren't many things that Hibernian and Hearts agree on, but the fact they both have histories written specifically about the post-war period and that these both have the same name has to tell us something. And while the respective sides never overlapped at their peaks, there was enough overlap in their reigns to ensure that Edinburgh was able to genuinely mount a sustained challenge to Glasgow dominance. What made this period even more 'golden' was that it wasn't just Edinburgh.

For 19 seasons, Scottish football was a place where clubs could rise and fall, where the trophies were shared around, and where the Old Firm duopoly was broken. Between 1946 and 1965, an astonishing 12 different clubs won at least one major trophy, with seven winning the league championship flag. This isn't to say the Old Firm disappeared, although it nearly did as Celtic were just a single defeat away from relegation in 1948. The post-World War Two era was something of a golden one for Rangers, who at that time were Scottish football's undisputed giants; in those 19 seasons of the post-war era, Rangers won ten Scottish championships, six League Cups and eight Scottish Cups, to add to their dominance of wartime football. But this makes the other clubs' achievements all the better as they took them on when they were strong. That Rangers team were known for their defence, which was rather topically nicknamed 'The Iron Curtain'. According to journalist John Rafferty who wrote *One Hundred Years of Scottish Football*, 'They played to a style which was not to the liking of spectators in general but it produced results for Rangers and that was all that was asked for by their followers.' They were formidable, but while a run of trophies like that would be viewed as domination in most other European countries, it was not the case in Scotland.

Aberdeen emerged from the war in good shape; they beat Hibernian in the final of the 1948 Scottish Cup and would go on to win their first championship flag in 1955. East Fife, from the small industrial town of Methil on Scotland's east coast, amazingly won the League Cup three times (1947/48, 1949/50, 1953/54), posted consecutive third-placed finishes in 1952 and 1953, and reached the final of the Scottish Cup (1949/50).[37] Motherwell, whose eponymous home town was an industrial hotspot in the west of Scotland, claimed both the League Cup (1950/51) and the Scottish Cup (1952), and Dundee, who were then the dominant of the two Dundee clubs, became the first club to retain the League Cup (1951/52 and 1952/53) as well as reaching the 1952 Scottish Cup Final and winning the league in 1962. Celtic clinched the league and Scottish Cup double (1953/54) and they would also win consecutive League Cups (1956/57 and 1957/58), and another Glasgow side, Clyde,[38] emerged to win the Scottish Cup in 1954/55 and 1957/58. Falkirk (1956/57) and St Mirren (1958/59) both won the Scottish Cup, and in what was to prove a portentous moment, a young manager called Jock Stein led his Dunfermline Athletic side to the Scottish Cup in 1961. And it wasn't just on the park that things were different since the war.

Part of the reason for the enormous crowds seen in the post-war period can be put down to the phenomenon of the 'Edinburgh' football fan. Countless interviewees talked about how they, or their dads, would go week about to Tynecastle and Easter Road. Big groups of friends and relatives, mixed between Hibbies and Hearts men, would meet every Saturday afternoon to go to the match. These are men for whom camaraderie had been all they had known for years; what did petty rivalries matter when you had been living so close to your own – and your mates' – mortality when fighting a war? And of course, these were still working men who didn't have a lot of time off. For many, work on a Saturday morning was followed by a *Seterday efternin* at the match with their relatives and mates, preceded and followed by a pint or two at their local. These men still had a team they supported, and I'm sure had their arguments and falling-outs among themselves, but not at the expense of their Saturday afternoon ritual; regardless of what club they supported, they wanted to be part of these golden years of Edinburgh *fitba*, and to this generation who had lost their youth to war rivalry wasn't high on their agenda. As Dave Mackay put in his autobiography when speaking of this era: 'Hibs and Hearts are arch enemies, always were and always will be, although the rivalry does not plumb the depths of the violent hatred felt between some Celtic and Rangers supporters. Or it didn't in my day.'

It was a point also made to me by football historian Andy Mitchell, who felt that the Edinburgh Derby was far less partisan than others, based on this post-war phenomenon and his own experiences of it. And legendary Hibernian captain Pat Stanton lamented in his autobiography that 'it's a great pity fans don't mix in the same way they did then [the 50s and 60s], going to each other's games and even standing together on the terraces at Derby games'. This post-war truce would have been helped by the fact that both teams were very much worth watching at this time, a fact reinforced by Stanton talking about how when he was a young man, he loved watching Alex Young of Hearts.

Hibernian, led by their visionary (at least by the standards of Scottish football) chairman Harry Swan and manager Willie McCartney, emerged from wartime football with the makings of a top team. While deemed 'unofficial', wartime football had carried on, and was even encouraged by the authorities to maintain morale, and no doubt to help clubs survive financially. With the great Matt Busby playing in their defence, and a young right-winger called Gordon Smith appearing in the side, Hibernian won the Southern League Cup[39] and the Summer Cup (two of the wartime cup competitions), and had started to form a rivalry with Rangers who were very dominant during the war years, winning all six wartime league competitions and appearing in all of the Southern League Cup finals. Hibernian finished runners-up in the league twice, and the two clubs played two Summer Cup finals, winning one apiece (Hibernian also lost a Summer Cup final to Partick Thistle). Rangers also beat Hibernian in the final of the Victory Cup (held to mark Victory in Europe), although Hibernian did score an astonishing 8-1 victory over Rangers in the Southern League, with a 16-year-old Gordon Smith scoring twice. It will come as a surprise to few that one of the factors behind Rangers' dominance of wartime football was, in the opinion of legendary football journalist Bob Crampsey, 'weak refereeing', with one *Daily Record* columnist cited by Crampsey writing that 'Rangers might not want favours from referees, but they certainly get them'. There was also much disquiet over how few Rangers players were called up (just two) while Hibernian and Motherwell had 30 and 13 called up respectively, according to journalist Andrew Smith writing in *The Scotsman* newspaper.

Smith went on to explain how Hearts did not enjoy the war years as much, and had concerns about finances from the outset of hostilities, although they did make the final of the Southern League Cup in 1940/41, losing to Rangers. The financial troubles, not to mention the trauma of losing their team, that Hearts had felt in World War One perhaps cast a long shadow. But just as Hibs laid

Heart of Midlothian FC's club crest, on the façade of the old main stand at Tynecastle Park

Hibernian FC's current badge, representing the different strands of their identity. The fact it is the fourth, possibly the sixth club crest reflects the difficulties they have had with their identity since they got rid of their original crest, the harp of Ireland with 'Ireland for ever' in Irish Gaelic, which was their badge and motto from their inception until the 1950s

The fully redeveloped Tynecastle Park, Hearts' home since 1886.

Tynecastle Park, right in the heart of Gorgie. To the bottom left of the stadium is the distillery (which used to cover the empty field as well) and the line of tenements running past the right of the stadium is Gorgie Road, the main street running through the area. Arthur's Seat and Edinburgh Castle are in the distance

Tynecastle Park from Gorgie Road, the area's high street.

The actual Heart of Midlothian mosaic, on the Royal Mile marks the site of the old city tollbooth and jail.

The Hearts memorial clock, at Haymarket in Edinburgh, with memorial wreaths from Hearts supporters' clubs at its base; and the memorial in Tynecastle Park. Both commemorate the Hearts team of 1914, who volunteered together to fight in the First World War

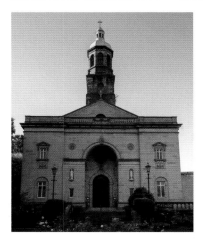

St Patrick's RC Church, in the Cowgate, the spiritual home of Hibernian FC

Easter Road, rising above its surrounding community. Leith and Leith docks are in the background

Easter Road, Hibernian's 'Holy Ground' since 1893

Hibernian supporters still revere the Famous Five, the club's most famous team which won three championships in five years in the 40s and 50s

Dave Mackay receiving the FA Cup as captain of Tottenham. A lifelong Hearts fan, he was the catalyst for Hearts' most successful period in the 1950s

The Cowgate
in the 19th
century, home to
Edinburgh's Irish
ghetto, from which
Hibernian FC
sprung

The Cowgate, modern
day underneath one of
the archways that carried
'respectable' Edinburgh
over the slums below

Hibernian fans quote
club legend Eddie
Turnbull as the teams
come out for a Derby
match in 2018;
'There's class, there's
first class and there's
Hibs class'

Hearts fans' display before the 2022 Scottish Cup Final versus Rangers.

Hearts fans getting ready to celebrate a Scottish Cup semi-final victory over Hibernian at Hampden Park, in 2022

Former Hearts owner Vladimir Romanov with the Scottish Cup won in 2012.

Hibernian supporters celebrate on the Hampden pitch after ending their 114-year Scottish Cup curse in 2016

down a marker in the war years that they would carry in to the resumption of 'normal' football, so too did Hearts, albeit in a different way, as Hearts upheld their honour by having the better of the local cup competitions. The maroons took four East of Scotland Shields (while the greens only managed three), and they held the upper hand in the Wilson Cup (by four to two), while the Rosebery Charity Cup was shared at three wins apiece. Although Hibernian had the better overall derby record during wartime football, winning 17 to Hearts' 13, with only six draws, Hearts did record a bizarre 6-5 victory at Easter Road in the Southern League, the background of which served as a potent reminder of the context in which the match was being played.

Thick fog had enveloped Easter Road, so much so that the BBC Radio commentator couldn't see the match. It resulted in him commentating for 105 minutes because he didn't realise the match had stopped. One of the Hearts players also made the same mistake, and stood on the pitch for ten minutes after his team-mates had gone in for their post-match baths. This was all confidential, because fog over the Forth was classified information (presumably the BBC continued as if nothing was wrong). This was for good reason, as the Firth of Forth was a target for the Luftwaffe, and indeed the first bombing raid of World War Two took place on the Royal Navy near the Forth Bridge just a couple of months prior to this match taking place. The RAF also recorded its first 'kill' of the entire war via the 603 (City of Edinburgh) Squadron.

The frequency with which the rivals played during the war reflected the localised nature of the competitions, and the need for gate receipts. And while the Edinburgh rivalry would continue back into league football, it would be the fledgling rivalry formed during the war between Hibernian and Rangers that would come to dominate the coming years, where attacking flair would come up against defensive solidity.

* * *

The brilliance of Hibernian's five-man forward line was built on genuinely innovative positional play, which often bamboozled the rigid defences of that era. Rafferty states: 'These five were immediately successful and they brought a new concept to Scottish football for they did not stick rigidly to set positions ... Hibs altered that thinking.'

The fluidity of their movement, and Scottish defences' inability to cope with it, built their reputation for brilliant attacking play. All five – Gordon Smith, Bobby Johnstone, Lawrie Reilly, Eddie Turnbull and Willie Ormond – would go on to score more than 100 league goals for the club, and together they were awarded more than 130 Scotland and Scottish league caps, and scored an astonishing 1,500 goals in total including 694 in the league. They are widely regarded as one of the best forward lines ever to emerge from Scotland (and even the UK). They won three championship flags in five years – 1947/48, 1950/51 and 1951/52 – and even more remarkably they came within one point (1949/50) and goal average (1952/53) of making it five titles in six seasons. Over this period they actually gained more league points and scored 113 more league goals than Rangers, and were the first non-Old Firm team to retain the league flag.[40] They almost certainly would have won more had it not been for the fact that their defence couldn't match the brilliance of their forwards, as described by Rafferty: 'Hibernian, a team of all the attacking graces, developed in Edinburgh and even in Glasgow there was admiration and envy of their forward line. There had been many famous Scottish club forward lines to slip off the tongue over the years … but none of them outshone Smith, Johnstone, Reilly, Turnbull and Ormond.'

Under the guidance of Swan, they were also very international in their outlook, touring abroad regularly as another example of Swan recognising the potential of societal advances (in this case, the aeroplane shrinking the world like never before). This led to Hibernian being invited to take part in an eight-team tournament, the Copa Rivadavia Correia Meyer Tournament, alongside Fluminense, Botafogo, Vasco da Gama, Corinthians, Sao Paulo, Sporting Club de Portugal (Sporting Lisbon) and Nacional (Uruguay). Hibs drew 3-3 with Vasco da Gama at the Maracana Stadium, but lost to both Botafogo and Fluminense.

Despite their brilliance, the Famous Five never managed to win a national cup competition, losing the Scottish Cup Final in 1947 and the League Cup Final in 1950/51. They also lost the Coronation Cup Final in 1953. This was a one-off tournament played to mark the coronation of Queen Elizabeth II and was a genuinely British tournament with entry by invitation. Hibernian burnished their credentials as one of the UK's top teams by defeating both Tottenham Hotspur (2-1 aet) and Newcastle United (4-0) on their way to the final where, despite being favourites, they lost to Celtic at Hampden; their old nemesis doing what *the famous English clubs* couldn't.[41]

* * *

The Famous Five's celebrity, partly brought about as a result of their European tours, led to them being invited to participate in the inaugural European Cup in 1955, becoming the first team from the UK to play in European competition. They managed to reach the semi-finals, disposing of Djurgardens of Sweden and Rot-Weiss Essen of West Germany before losing to the French side Stade de Reims. The Famous Five were denied their moment in history and a stab at Real Madrid, who would go on and win the first of five consecutive European Cup titles.

The golden post-war era of Scottish football would continue even as the lustre of the Famous Five diminished. But just as they faded, Hearts emerged from their shadow and started to fulfil the potential of their own formidable forward line that became known as 'The Terrible Trio'. As Eddie Turnbull, the inside-left in the Famous Five, put it in his autobiography:

Alfie Conn, Jimmy Wardhaugh and Willie Bauld were all magnificent footballers and were the driving force which propelled Hearts ... We got on well with them off the pitch, but there was an intense rivalry between the two Edinburgh clubs then as now, and there was nothing we liked more than beating Hearts in a Ne'erday Derby. Which actually didn't happen all that often.

The Terrible Trio had in fact been around since the late 40s (they first played together in 1948), but despite their attacking talents, they never quite managed to transition to winning competitions, and they had a reputation for playing nice, if not winning, football. They also laboured under the weight of history, with it approaching nearly 50 years since Hearts had won a national trophy, a source of embarrassment to the club (and much mirth to the rest of Scottish football) given their early history. According to Hearts historian Norrie Price, the club's nice-but-harmless image soon ended when they put in place a half-back line to match their 'rapier-like Tynecastle attack'. Freddie Glidden, John Cumming and Dave Mackay were every bit as important as their illustrious Terrible Trio colleagues, and together they formed one of the most formidable and complete sides Scottish football has ever seen.

Hearts had been showing signs of promise in the cups, but had been unable to find the consistency to challenge Hibernian and Rangers for the league title. But while they may have been in their rivals' shadow in terms of the league, they were building a strong record in the head-to-heads, showing their potential, including two seasons – 1949/50 and 1950/51 – when Hearts won both league derby matches – one a 5-2 thumping at Tynecastle in September 1949. In the three national competitions, Hearts won ten victories versus Hibernian's five, although the greens did also reel off five consecutive East of Scotland Shield victories from 1947 to 1953. But as Hibernian fell away, Hearts asserted themselves in the derby to a far greater extent than their rivals had managed during their heyday. In the years from season 1953/54 to 1964/65, Hearts won 26 derby matches to Hibernian's 14 (with five draws).[42] This spell began with Hearts putting together eight derby victories in a row between 1953 and 1955, including consecutive 5-0 and 5-1 victories; this was truly an era of derby dominance, with Hearts also winning the East of Scotland Shield six times versus five for Hibernian.

Hearts finally ended their 48-year wait for a national trophy when they defeated Motherwell in the 1954 League Cup Final, and this win acted like the unlocking of a dam, as described by Mackie:

> 'No longer would comics bring the roof down by equating 'the time Hearts won the cup' with 'the year of the short corn'. Even though it was the League Cup, and not the Scottish Cup, a bogy had been dispelled, and a time-honoured but tasteless joke had been killed stone dead.'

The Scottish Cup followed in 1956 when Hearts defeated Celtic 3-1 in the final, a result that saw enormous crowds take to the streets of Edinburgh to welcome home their conquering heroes after nearly 50 years of waiting. Worryingly for the rest, this team hadn't reached its peak yet and better was to come in the 1957/58 season, when Hearts became Scottish champions for the first time since 1897. Hearts didn't just win the league that season, they absolutely steamrollered it, scoring a record 132 goals and winning by 13 points from second-placed Rangers (with just two points for a win) and losing just one game all season. It is undoubtedly one of the greatest ever league seasons put together by a Scottish side, and it put Hearts back at the top of Scottish football for the first time since the turn of the century.

Fittingly for the Edinburgh rivalry, it was Hibernian who, against the odds, ended Hearts' hope of a league and cup double by going to Tynecastle and surprisingly winning 4-3 to put Hearts out of the Scottish Cup. Young striker Joe Baker, just 17 at the time, scored all four of Hibs' goals, and fevered talk of an Edinburgh double arose in the media. Unfortunately for them, Hibs' Scottish Cup curse, this time in the form of Clyde, struck again and they were defeated in the final.

Hearts followed up their championship flag with the League Cup in season 1958/59, easily beating Partick Thistle 5-1 in the final, although it was to be a bittersweet season, as Hearts surprisingly (and against his wishes and obviously to the dismay of their supporters) sold captain Dave Mackay to Tottenham Hotspur for £32,000. In his absence, Hearts still went on to retain the League Cup in

1959/60 before adding another championship to complete the league and League Cup double.

It is worth noting that a member of the Hearts league and League Cup-winning team was none other than 'The Prince of Wingers', Gordon Smith, who had been released by Hibernian because he was too old and too injured (Hibernian, in a style indicative of the high-handed way they sometimes dealt with players in those days, refused to pay for a second ankle operation – a shabby way to treat one of their greatest ever players and a servant of 18 years). Neither age nor injury prevented him from winning the league and League Cup with Hearts, although incredibly, after he was released by Hearts, he went on to win the league again, this time with Dundee, in 1961/62. Smith's haul of five Scottish championship medals with three different clubs (none of them the Old Firm) is a feat that will never be repeated and must surely put him right up there as one of the greatest Scottish players ever; he has been inducted into the Hibernian and Dundee Halls of Fame, Scottish Sports Hall of Fame and the Scottish Football Hall of Fame. He was also the inaugural winner of the Rex Kingsley Footballer of the Year award in 1951, a prize that became quite prestigious (and was subsequently won by both Dave Mackay and John Cumming of Hearts in 1958 and 1961 respectively).[43]

Dave Mackay would famously go on to become a key member of the double-winning Spurs team in 1961, claim the FA Cup on a further two occasions and the European Cup Winners' Cup in 1962/63, before going on to succeed none other than the great Brian Clough as manager of Derby County, leading them to the league title in 1975.

Winning those titles meant that Hearts could follow Hibernian into the European Cup. Their campaign in 1958 was a disappointing one, however, and they couldn't match their great rivals' earlier success, as they lost to Standard Liege 6-3 on aggregate, after losing the first leg in Belgium 5-1. In 1960 Hearts were again representing Scotland in the European Cup, but were unlucky to draw Portuguese champions Benfica, who were about to become European royalty themselves. Benfica easily won both legs to take the tie 5-1 on aggregate, as they went on to win the trophy, then retain it the following season.

Throughout this period Rangers had remained the team to beat, and they started the 60s by claiming the cup double in season 1961/62, the league and cup double in 1962/63 and the treble in 1963/64, an ominous sign that their power was rising, but there was time for one last hurrah for the 'other guys' in 1964/65. Hibernian, after years of doing nothing much apart from one disastrous season in 1963 that almost ended in relegation, had enjoyed a sudden renaissance under Jock Stein, and were in the title race along with Hearts. Despite flying high in the league and in the semi-finals of the Scottish Cup with just a few weeks to go, they were hobbled when Stein left to take over as Celtic manager. This left behind a huge sense of 'what if' at Easter Road, made all the worse by the fact that Stein led his new charges to the very same Scottish Cup he had a good chance of winning with Hibernian. Hibs fans were convinced that had he stayed, they would have won one, if not both, of those trophies. In the end they had to watch as Hearts and Kilmarnock fought for the flag.

Hearts were way past their peak by this point, but they did win their fourth League Cup in eight seasons when they defeated Kilmarnock 2-1 in 1962/63. And they looked like they had done enough to win another league title, only needing to avoid a two-goal defeat at Tynecastle on the last day of the season. But their closest rivals, Kilmarnock, were, by brilliant happenstance, to be the visitors on that last day; a proper, one-match, title shoot-out. Amazingly, Kilmarnock got the exact result they needed, a 2-0 victory, and pipped Hearts on goal average (had it been goal difference, Hearts would have won) and, in doing so, got revenge for their earlier League Cup Final defeat at the hands of Hearts. Kilmarnock were generally deemed worthy champions, having finished runners-up in four of the previous five seasons, but for Hearts it was a golden opportunity missed, a rare chance to win the league flag; although I doubt at the time that fans would have realised just how rare a chance it was to prove to be.

For as wonderful as that league win must have been for Kilmarnock in 1965, the most significant moment for the wider Scottish game took place at Hampden Park, where the newly installed manager of Celtic, Jock Stein, led his club to its first trophy in seven years by winning the Scottish Cup. His brilliance, and that of the team he quickly assembled at Celtic Park, killed off the post-war era of competitiveness stone dead. The Old Firm reasserted dominance over the Scottish game, with Celtic rising to become the best team in Europe in 1967 and the Old Firm sharing the next 14 league titles (including Celtic winning nine in a row). In the 58 seasons since that day, 54 of the titles have gone to Parkhead or Ibrox, with only Aberdeen (three times) and Dundee United (once) being the lucky clubs to break that monopoly. The post-war boom faded, the record crowds that saw every ground bursting at the seams ebbed, the post-World War Two spirit of camaraderie and keen but sporting rivalry disappeared. Just as society moved from black and white austerity into the swinging 60s, so too did Scottish football supporters, who fell back into tribal support fuelled by drunkenness, and often ending in violence. That league decider at Tynecastle in 1965 was to be the requiem for Edinburgh football's golden years, as well as for Scottish football's post-war boom.

CHAPTER 12

HIBERNIAN DOMINATION

1966–1979

THE HEARTBREAKING loss of the league championship on the final day of the season was a watershed moment for Hearts, and it hit them hard, so hard in fact that they took 20 years to really recover. One historian of the club, J. Fairgrieve, estimated that Hearts lost half their support as a result of that calamitous loss, 'for that title was lost badly, by unimaginative tactics, to a team who couldn't have been more astonished by success'. For the first time since the 1880s, Hibernian would dominate their city rivals, and maintain their place towards the top of Scottish football for a prolonged period; in fact, in the 70s Hibernian were undoubtedly Scotland's third force. It was a period that, for Hibernian, would be defined by a seemingly constant tussle with the Old Firm. It is ironic that years later, Vladimir Romanov would dismiss Hibernian as not real rivals, only to have his period defined by matches against them. Hibernian would have been delighted to have Hearts as a rival in the 70s, but the fates ensured that they genuinely were fighting the Old Firm rather than their neighbours. Between 1968 and 1979, Hibernian would play in five major cup finals, and two more minor cup finals, and in all of them they came up against the Old Firm; Celtic, in their Jock Stein nine-in-a-row pomp, were their opponents six times in seven finals, Rangers in the other one. However, they did have an unhappy knack of playing Rangers in semi-finals (there was always a suspicion among non-Old Firm fans that Rangers and Celtic were kept apart until cup finals by the powers-that-be in their closed, wood-panelled, smoke-filled rooms).

For Hearts, it was a period of struggle, with a solitary fourth place being the highest they would finish in the league until season 1985/86. These years were so bad that the mediocre seasons were the highlight, as Hearts slipped into becoming a yo-yo club in the mid-70s, and at one point looked likely to go part-time, or even disappear completely. In the four seasons after the 1965/66 season, Hearts slumped in the league, and also lost in the Scottish Cup Final to Dunfermline Athletic. They would reach another Scottish Cup Final in 1976, and the match kicked off early, meaning Hearts became the only team to concede a goal before the 3pm kick-off time in a Scottish Cup Final after Rangers scored in the first minute, on their way to winning. Their relegation in 1977 was the first in Hearts' history, and was a huge blow to their prestige, as well as to their finances.

Hibernian on the other hand started to fly, finishing the 60s with two third-place finishes and a League Cup Final appearance (and a what was to become habitual hammering from Celtic, by 6-2) in the 1968/69 season. The greens dropped off in 1970/71, finishing in mid-table, before going on a run that saw them mount a challenge for the title in the following years; finishing fourth, third, second, second and third. This was consistency by anyone's standards, never mind Hibernian's notoriously up-and-down style.

The team earned the nickname of 'Turnbull's Tornadoes' (named after legendary former player Eddie Turnbull, who had returned as manager) in honour of their attacking style of play. As their cup final results will testify, however, they did have a habit of leaving the back door ajar. As well as the 1968/69 League Cup Final, Hibernian lost 6-1 to Celtic in the 1972 Scottish Cup Final (having beaten Rangers in the semi-final), and amazingly shipped six again in the 1974/75 League Cup Final, losing 6-3 (Hibernian forward Joe Harper scored a hat-trick in a losing cup final). Hibernian did beat Celtic in two Drybrough Cup[44] finals, winning 5-3 in 1972 and 1-0 in 1973 (and, of course, Hibernian had defeated Rangers in both semi-finals).[45] The Tornadoes' high point, however, did come against Celtic, when Hibernian defeated them in the 1972 League Cup Final, winning 2-1, with local boys and Hibernian supporters Pat Stanton and Jimmy O'Rourke scoring the goals. Amazingly this was Hibernian's first major cup (as opposed to league titles and minor or wartime cup competitions) victory since their Scottish Cup win in 1902.

That was a golden period for Hibernian, who followed up their cup final victory with an 8-1 league win over Ayr

United. And just a few weeks later, Hibernian went to Tynecastle on New Year's Day and defeated Hearts 7-0. It was a seismic defeat for Hearts, emblematic of how far they had fallen behind their city rivals. It was the low point of a long run of Hibernian superiority in the derby. Between the start of season 1966/67 and 1979, Hearts only won six matches (only three of which were league fixtures, three being in the East of Scotland Shield). It was Hibernian's greatest era of derby dominance, and included a run of 12 matches undefeated in league and cups from 1974 to 1978. Hearts were probably fortunate that there were only two derbies a season rather than four for most of this era, and cup meetings were rare; in fact they were only drawn together in the Scottish Cup twice, Hibernian winning both ties 2-1. It must be frustrating for Hibernian fans that they didn't face them more often in the cups in this era.

This team also made their mark in Europe, continuing a tradition Hibernian had begun with their run to the European Cup semi-final in 1955, and the Fairs Cup (which later became the UEFA Cup) semi-final in 1960 (Hibernian would have won that semi had away goals counted at the time, drawing 2-2 with AS Roma at home and 3-3 with them away). In 1967/68, Hibernian defeated Porto, before facing Napoli in the next round. They lost in Naples 4-1, and the tie looked dead. But in a quite astonishing second leg at Easter Road, Hibernian won 5-0 to go through and set up a 'battle of Britain' against Leeds United, which Leeds won 2-1 on aggregate. In this period Hibernian played Hamburg (losing on away goals), Valencia (twice, losing both ties), Malmo (winning 9-2 on aggregate), Sporting Lisbon (winning 7-3 on aggregate, including inflicting Sporting's heaviest ever European defeat, winning by 6-1 at Easter Road), Rosenborg, Juventus and others. They also played Liverpool twice and Leeds United again (losing on penalties). These European nights hold a special place in folklore for Hibernian supporters, and were another factor in building the legend of great Hibernian forwards, playing great attacking football.

The Tornadoes' era did come to an end, and Hibernian slipped to mid-table in 1977, where they remained until they were relegated in 1980. As much as the 1970s was a golden era, the 80s was to be a dismal one for Hibernian. There was an epic, three-match Scottish Cup Final against Rangers in 1979, which Hibs eventually lost 3-2 in the second replay.

Their legacy to Hibernian is a double-edged one. While they were a brilliant and exciting team, and they were definitely unlucky to come up against the Old Firm at a time when both were particularly strong,[46] they also took some hammerings, particularly from Celtic in those cup finals. If the Famous Five were responsible for laying out a Hibernian style with their innovative attacking play in the late 40s and early 50s, then the Tornadoes (and the mercurial teams of the 60s, which could be brilliant but were painfully inconsistent) cemented it as something to which all Hibernian teams – and supporters – must aspire. This has meant that ever since, Hibernian and their supporters have wrestled with the rights and wrongs of footballing styles and approaches, almost certainly to their detriment. Even today, there are many who would rather watch an ultra-attacking approach (with the inconsistency that is inherent in such teams) than have a manager put in place a solid foundation and build a strong team. To some this is romantic and idealistic, and in keeping with Hibernian's broader identity. To others, it is conceited and unrealistic, thinking that Hibernian can achieve success without putting in the hard yards of building a side that can defend properly. That debate continues to rage among the Hibernian supporters to this day, and more than one manager has been hounded out by fans for being 'too dull'. It is hard not to draw a very short, very straight line between this belief and Hibernian's perennial inconsistency and unreliability, as building a competitive and consistent team from the front is almost impossible.

For Hibernian this was the last great era, and while a taste of it was reprised for a brief couple of seasons under Tony Mowbray in the mid-2000s, there is a sense that this kind of era – battling with top English clubs, hammering teams in Europe, regularly competing with and beating the Old Firm – is gone forever. And while that team were decried for their inconsistency, they did finish in the top four in seven out of nine seasons, including twice being runners-up, with three third-place finishes and two fourth-place finishes, while reaching four major cup finals. How they would love to be that inconsistent again.

And what did this era do to Hearts and their supporters? Edina's Darlings were languishing way behind their rivals in every sphere, and their crowds plummeted, bringing in an existential crisis that could have seen the club go out of business. To a club and fanbase built on the rock-solid belief that they were 'the superior club', this must have been very hard to accept. And while they did bounce back in the mid-80s, it is hard not to wonder if their takeover attempt in 1990 was in some way linked to the loss of prestige that they suffered in this era.

CHAPTER 13

HEARTS DOMINANCE

1980–1990

AS HEARTS fans faced their third promotion in five years in 1983, few, if any, of them would have thought that by the time the decade finished, they would be in the middle of a period of utter dominance in the derby. To paraphrase a famous football cliché, it was a decade of two halves for Hearts. For Hibernian, it was a dark era that started badly, and got gradually worse, which is ironic as the early 1980s are seen as something of a mini golden age in Scottish football, although the extent to which the Old Firm dominance was challenged by the 'New Firm'[47] has been exaggerated. The reality was Dundee United won the League Cup back-to-back in 1979/80 and 1980/81, and the league title in 1982/83.[48] Aberdeen on the other hand won three league championships, five Scottish Cups, three League Cups, the European Cup Winners' Cup and the European Super Cup; a true golden era. But the Old Firm won the rest of the trophies, as we will see.

As the 1980s began, Hearts were still enduring the worst era in their history. The mid-1960s to the late 1970s had seen Hibernian assert themselves as the dominant team in the city; always an uncomfortable position for Hearts to find themselves in. And that sense of decline, the stagnation and decay of a once mighty Edinburgh institution was to reach its low point as Hearts fell into their yo-yo years, bouncing between the Premier League (top league) and the First Division (second league) in a manner that was as unlikely as it was unpalatable to one of the great clubs of Scottish football, a point made by journalist Alan Pattullo in *The Scotsman*:

> Yo-yo club is not a phrase one might necessarily associate with Hearts but a league table has been doing the rounds this week which suggests this description is partly merited … that's now five times Hearts have suffered this fate [relegation] since reconstruction in 1975. Only Dundee … have endured a higher number [with seven].

Hearts went down for the first time in their history in season 1976/77 (two teams from a league of ten were relegated, a particularly cut-throat set-up), won promotion in 1977/78, went back down in 1978/79 but bounced back again in 1979/80, only to finish bottom of the league again in 1980/81, this time spending two years in the second league before winning promotion in the 1982/83 season. This time they managed to consolidate, and started to build. As they had navigated their way around some of the less glamorous grounds in the country and faced the realistic prospect of turning part-time, Hearts fans couldn't have thought they were about to witness a renaissance and rebuild their reputation under new owner Wallace Mercer. In hindsight, the return of Hearts was a story both made in, and very much of, the 1980s. A smooth-talking self-publicist, who was unashamedly capitalist and who was barely even a football fan, came out of nowhere, awash with big ideas.

Hibernian hit their own watershed moment with the second relegation in their history in 1980 – despite (or perhaps because of) having an ageing, unhealthy George Best in their team. This marked the end of a steady decline under manager Eddie Turnbull, and while Hibernian bounced back straightaway, and reached an unlikely League Cup Final in 1985 (beating both Celtic and Rangers on the way, before losing to Aberdeen), it was an era of mediocrity at best. Their relegation in 1980 also meant there was a hiatus in the normal derby matches, as both clubs missed each other in the top flight. This break ended Hibernian's era of derby dominance, and ushered in an Edinburgh Derby golden era for Hearts.

'I never understood how my dad was so confident ahead of derbies,' admits Jamie, a Hibernian fan whose school years spanned the 80s and 90s. 'He was always so relaxed, and seemed so unconcerned. Partly I think it was just being a bit older and having been around the block. But also, I think that growing up in a period when things were either even, and then when Hibs were the top dogs meant he didn't fear derbies in the same way. He'd never had to!' The apprehension that Jamie talks about is prevalent in many Hibernian fans from that era, and the mirror image comes across quickly with Hearts fans. They just knew they were the better team when it came to derbies. Partly this was because, for most of the 80s, Hearts were just the better team, but there was something more.

The season Hearts were promoted again in 1983, they went on a run of 17 derbies undefeated. For a club who had been under the boot of their rival since the mid-60s, it was a radical turnaround in fortunes, and the perfect response to the indignity of the yo-yo years. In fact, Hearts' dominance of the derby in the 80s was such that, between 1980 and 1990, they lost to their derby rivals only three times, a remarkable record, especially when you consider these years included playing each other four times a season in the league.[49] Looking at the results, what really stands out is how close the results were; of those 17 matches, eight were draws. Of the nine victories, seven of them were by a single goal, and the other two were by two goals.

This might sound like a criticism, but on the contrary, this is what the derby dominance was built on, and what made it all the more remarkable. Hearts were a better team for most of those years, but not by that great a margin. But they managed to find a way not to lose, and to sneak wins even when they didn't deserve to; they were psychological wins as much as they were about playing talent, and the narrowness of so many of these results helped to build an X factor, a sense of impregnability about Hearts going into derbies. Fans can accept when their team gets walloped by a much better team, but losing (or not winning) tight matches by tight margins made it worse for the Hibernian fans, and better for the Hearts fans. Because it wasn't about playing well, and they knew that it didn't really matter how their general form was, or how they played in a particular match, they believed they wouldn't lose, and Hibernian probably doubted that they would win, that they would get the breaks. Wallace Mercer, the Hearts chairman, admitted that 'luck had been mostly on our side for years in the Edinburgh Derby'. And nobody embodied this more than John Robertson, the 'Hammer of Hibs'.

'If ever there was a fixture I revelled in, it was the derby,' Robertson said years later. History will judge it as one of the most catastrophic mistakes Hibernian ever made; on such tiny cogs, the wheels of football history turn, and as is often the case with these stories it could have all been so different. Robertson had agreed terms with Hibernian to join their youth system after meeting Eddie Turnbull and Pat Stanton. He was happy, but his brother (acting as his adviser as his father had passed away) had told him not to sign anything until he had looked it over. The trouble was his brother played for Rangers at the time, as he recalled in his autobiography:

> I informed Tom Hart (the Hibernian chairman) and the management that everything seemed in order and that once Chris had looked it over I would be happy to sign it and bring it back the following evening ... 'No' he said. 'I don't want

the details going out of this room and I don't want anyone working with Rangers to see it. You have to sign that document now or not at all.' ... Tom Hart, I was told years later, did not really like Rangers or anything to do with them and I can only think that was the reason.

He signed for Hearts instead. To call it a costly mistake wouldn't do it justice. A costly mistake was Hibernian not signing Gordon Strachan, despite being a local lad and a Hibby. Losing out on Robbo and his going to the direct rivals could have been a costly mistake had he just had a normal career, but he went on to have a legendary career, becoming Hearts' all-time top goalscorer and, most relevantly for this story, becoming their all-time top scorer against Hibernian, and the top scorer in the Edinburgh Derby. And he did this at – and heavily contributed to – a time when Hearts built an incredible dominance.

Hearts weren't purely focused on beating their rivals, however, and in season 1985/86 they made an unlikely assault on the league championship. It was Hearts' interjection into the era of the New Firm, after Aberdeen had just equalled Hibernian's Famous Five in winning back-to-back titles in 1984 and 1985, and Dundee United had won their first and only league title in 1983.

Led by manager Alex MacDonald, Hearts built a competitive and hard-working team, who had a couple of players capable of magic in John Colquhoun and John Robertson, and they went on a charge that put them in the driving seat for the title and made it to their first Scottish Cup Final in ten years by defeating Dundee United in the semi-final. With just three matches left, Hearts had a five-point lead over Dundee United and Celtic; they needed just four points from their final three matches, and they would clinch their fifth ever championship title. A nervy but battling 1-1 draw with Aberdeen was followed by an even more nervy 1-0 victory over Clydebank, and with three points secured (it was only two points for a win in those days) they needed just one more. An unbeaten run of 27 league matches (31 in all competitions) was testament to their resilience, and they just needed one more draw. Celtic, who had come from nine points back to close the gap to just two, also had an inferior goal difference and required a four-goal swing as well as Hearts losing. For the 10,000 Hearts fans inside Dundee's Dens Park they had gone to see a title party, and who could blame them – only a catastrophic set of results could derail them.

The match was 0-0 at half-time, but the news filtered through from Paisley, where Celtic were playing St Mirren, that the Glasgow giants had scored three goals in five minutes, and within five minutes of half-time Celtic were four up, but as long as Hearts got a point it didn't matter how many Celtic scored. Hearts went defensive to try and see things out, but it didn't work. Dundee scored with just seven minutes remaining, and then again four minutes later to give the Dark Blues a 2-0 victory. Celtic had hammered St Mirren 5-0 to steal the title from Hearts: 'At the final whistle, the Hearts players and officials were devastated and there were heart-rending scenes amongst the Gorgie faithful, who were stunned that their dreams of glory had been so cruelly shattered.'[50]

The following week Hearts lost the Scottish Cup Final to Aberdeen, 3-0. The 1980s was a difficult period in which to win trophies, with Dundee United and particularly Aberdeen being so strong. In saying that, both St Mirren and Motherwell managed to win the Scottish Cup (in 1987 and 1991 respectively), but Aberdeen dominated it in the 80s, winning five Scottish Cups between 1982 and 1990. And as the decade wore on, Rangers, flush with investment, awoke from their own dark years, winning their first league title of the decade in 1987, and from 1989 winning nine titles in a row. Hearts remained competitive, finishing second in 1988 and third in 1990, but they never got that close to winning a trophy again; they had blown their chance and wouldn't even make a cup final again until the mid-90s, developing a difficult relationship with semi-finals. Hibernian were even less competitive, bobbing about in mid-table, despite being taken over and having a brief moment when it looked like they might regain their place challenging at the top of Scottish football. They did manage to briefly interrupt Hearts' derby dominance, going six league derby matches undefeated (three wins, three draws), but it is a sign of how bleak things were that this is the high point of that decade for the greens, and Hearts did manage a 5-1 East of Scotland Shield victory during that run.

The routine of four league derby matches a season, brought in with the league reorganisation in 1975, had proved to be saturation point for the derby. The local cup competitions, which had started to fade in the 70s when Hibernian twice declined to enter, fell away completely with attendances for the matches plummeting. The East of Scotland Shield (formerly the Edinburgh FA Cup, and then the Edinburgh Shield) was eventually made a youth tournament in 1990, which is still played for today. For the record, the final tally up until 1989/90 was Hibernian with 49 victories and Hearts with 48.[51] One of the lessons I have learned in writing this book is not to be so dismissive of the minor/local competitions. In those early years, the Edinburgh FA Cup was effectively Hearts' and Hibernian's domestic championship, and carried huge importance. And even as it lost some of its prominence with the advent of the Scottish League in 1890, and the League Cup after World War Two, at a time when the clubs only met twice a year in the league there was space in the calendar for the fixture to retain its significance. It's not clear why the Edinburgh Derby league matches cannot still be used to work out who wins the various local trophies throughout Scotland, which once carried such significance – in the way that Edinburgh and Glasgow rugby teams double up their league fixtures as the 1872 Cup.

As the decade came to a close, Hearts could not have known that a 2-1 victory (John Robertson scoring the winner in the 81st minute) in April 1989 would kick off an even better run of undefeated derby matches; and nobody could have known how the new decade would see the Edinburgh Derby altered for a generation. Any thoughts about what might have been in the recent past or what may be about to happen in the coming years were to be brushed aside by a series of incredible events. Hearts were going to try and buy Hibernian.

CHAPTER 14

THE TEAM THAT
WOULDN'T DIE

IT WAS the close season, and there was no match taking place, but the east terracing at Easter Road was packed. A large marquee was on the pitch, and the mood was sombre, almost funereal. Joe Baker, the legendary Hibernian striker, walked forward with a Hibernian scarf raised aloft. He got down on both knees, bent forward and kissed the turf before standing back up and taking an emotional acclaim from the fans who had worshipped him. At the mic he said Hibernian would not die, and that this great club would rise from the ashes like a phoenix.

What was the threat that provoked such fatalistic language? Hearts had launched a hostile takeover bid, and were attempting to shut Hibernian down. It was an extraordinary time, a move almost unparalleled in modern football history, certainly in the UK.[52]

Oftentimes history serves to clarify things, stripping away the stories and smokescreens to reveal actual events and the motivations of those behind them. But sometimes it does the opposite, and layers of myth, false memories and revision are added to an event, usually because of the way it turned out, or what the 'optics' of it have become. Wallace Mercer was the undoubted villain of the piece, no doubt about that; it was his vision, his arrogance. But he has also become a lightning rod, allowing people to talk about the takeover in a way that feels safe to be written off as the misadventures of an eccentric. It's now classed and discussed more as a 'merger'. This piece, on news website Edinburgh Live by J. Delaney, is a good example:

> The £6.2 million offer for the financially stricken Easter Road side was part of a plan to merge the club with their Tynecastle rivals and move a new 'Edinburgh United' to a stadium on the outskirts of the city.

This makes sense from a media point of view; it is easier for them and it means they don't have to be seen to be taking sides. But there was no talk of Edinburgh United anywhere from Mercer. Instead, the offer documents state that it was a cash offer by 'Heart of Midlothian Football Club plc for Edinburgh Hibernian plc'. The offer was put forward by Bell Lawrie White & Co. Limited and Macdonald Orr Corporate Finance Limited on behalf of Heart of Midlothian Football Club plc.

This wasn't a merger, it was a takeover.

Easter Road was to be sold straightaway and the 'new' club were to play at Tynecastle, in maroon and be called Heart of Midlothian, until a new ground could be built in the west of the city. Mercer was fond of PR; he was a self-publicist who loved the media and went out of his way to build his media profile. It seems unlikely that such a media-savvy man would not have thought about how to publicly present his takeover attempt, how to spin things to increase the chances of his success, and to minimise the backlash.

While Hibernian cannot be blamed for the takeover attempt, they can certainly be blamed for making themselves so vulnerable in the first place. And just as Wallace Mercer was a figure very much of his time, so was Hibernian's demise. Taken over in 1987 by David Duff, a Hibernian fan, all seemed well. Hibernian floated shares which the fans lapped up, and even spent some money, signing Andy Goram from Oldham Athletic in England and, amazingly, signing Steve Archibald (the rumour was that Hibs offered more money than Liverpool!). But it wasn't like they went mad signing superstars, as was reflected in their league positions. Hibs had got better – they even managed to win a couple of derby matches. But it was what was going on behind the scenes that was laying the foundations for trouble.

It turned out that Duff had been loaned the money by another man, David Rowland – which made him effectively Hibernian's owner. The share issue rewarded both Rowland and Duff, and Rowland's loan was repaid at an eye-watering interest rate. As Hibernian historian John Mackay pointed out, in effect Hibernian fans had paid for Duff and Rowland to own the club (a bit like the Glazers at Manchester United) at almost no cost to themselves. Hibernian then bought a pub in Exeter –

ironically called the Talk of the Town[53] – and a sports and country club in Devon. Alarm bells really started to ring when Hibernian bought a chain of pubs in the south-west of England for £5.75m (the club itself had only been valued at £4m). This chain had sprung out of another chain of pubs that had gone bust, owing money to a company called London and Suburban Land, who at that time had a director called Jeremy James; the first two pubs Hibs bought had also been bought out of receivership, after James's company had pulled the plug on them. Jeremy James was now sitting on the Hibernian board, having come in with the new regime.

Even more worryingly, Avon Inns was a loss-making arm of a company called Inoco. Inoco were owned by David Rowland, the man who had lent Duff the money to buy Hibernian; effectively the owner of the club. He was using one part of his business empire to buy unprofitable bits from the other parts. Despite assurances to the contrary, the pub chain made a loss of £1.6m in its first year, while at the same time, through other financial slights of hand, Rowland sold his personal shares in the club (at 100 per cent profit because he had gifted them to himself), while increasing his ownership through his company, which had also diluted Duff's and the supporters' share of ownership. Hibernian were now owned by uninterested investors, and making big losses. The sad irony of it for Hibs fans is that most clubs who get into financial difficulties do so by buying players they can't afford, and living the dream for a short while. While Hibernian did spend a bit more cash than normal on

Steve Archibald and a couple of others, this was no lavish spending spree where the team burned brightly for a high point before collapsing in on itself. In what was described to me as 'typical Hibs', Hibs got themselves into financial trouble not by buying great players, but by buying shite pubs; the end result was the same though.

This is where Mercer and Hearts came in. Some Edinburgh businessmen approached him on hearing that Hibernian might be available to buy, with the idea of a friendly merger between the two clubs put to him (how friendly that would have been is obviously open for debate). Mercer rebuffed that idea, but took the knowledge that Hibernian's shareholders were open to a sale to develop his own approach, and launched the hostile takeover. The vision he sold was for a single Edinburgh club to take on the Old Firm. John Mackay states: 'Unfortunately that meant the end of Hibs and the closure of Easter Road, but that was the price of progress.'

The city awoke to the news of the deal, that 'Hibs had played their last game at Easter Road, that the ground would be closed and that the capital's football would in future be concentrated in a super Hearts club'. No merger, no Edinburgh United, no jeopardy for Hearts.

The Hibernian fan reaction was furious, and a campaign – 'Hands Off Hibs' – was launched. It quickly gathered momentum, helped by huge media coverage; this was a massive story, one club trying to impose a hostile takeover on their city rivals. John Leslie, a TV presenter and Hibernian fan, even wore a Hands Off Hibs T-shirt on *Blue*

Peter, one of the most popular children's TV programmes on BBC1. The main BBC news led with the story, and a petition was handed into Downing Street by local MPs.

But Hibernian's fault in the past had been naivety, and while the Hands Off Hibs campaign was heavy on the soft power aspects, public opinion wasn't going to sway this. David Duff admirably refused to sell his shares, but Mercer had over 60 per cent of the shares pledged to him. Hands Off Hibs needed some hard power and they managed to convince two businessmen, former owner Kenny Waugh (who Mercer had beaten to win the ownership of Hearts back in 1981) and Tom Farmer, to buy shares as a blocking move. Once they did that, Mercer was checked, as the Bank of Scotland finance was dependent upon him securing 76 per cent of shares. Mercer began to wobble, and even tried to rescue his deal by offering Hibernian the chance to stay in existence, and then join Hearts at their new stadium at Hermiston Gate (which perhaps spoke to his real motives).

There was another form of hard power that may or may not have had some influence on his decision-making. One interviewee for this book told me a story from that time:

> My next-door neighbour at the time was in Lothian and Borders Police, and he told me he was on duty outside Mercer's home one night during the takeover attempt, when a van load of Hibs casuals pulled up outside. Because he was a local copper and also a Hibby, he knew who they were – there were some well-kent faces. He told

me they had a milk crate full of petrol bombs, and he was in no doubt what they were there to do. He managed to talk them down and turn the van around before anything happened, or any of his colleagues noticed and tried to arrest them.

Such stories are obviously impossible to verify, although it is worth noting that Mercer himself did cite the threats of violence to him and his family, including receiving a bullet in the post, as stated in the *Edinburgh Evening News*: 'The Mercer [family] reveal the colourful businessman had also become concerned for his family's safety, his children having to be escorted to school while he and his wife were subject to death threats.' A former Hibs casual, interviewed in a *Daily Record* article in May 2020 and who has since released a memoir, indicated that his gang plotted against Mercer after he tried to take over Hibs in 1989: 'I am not saying we would have killed him but we had contingency plans to do him serious harm.'

In the end Mercer withdrew his bid when it was clear he couldn't proceed, or that it might not be worth it to him personally. Hibernian had won, but now faced a battle with their terrible finances. Tom Farmer eventually bought the club, reprising his family's role as Hibernian white knights. Both his grandfather and great-uncle had been among the Leith Hibernian community who had got the club back on its feet after its financial troubles in 1890. That it was again his family saving Hibernian, despite not being interested in football, was fitting.

Mercer's motivations will never be fully known, as he died of cancer in 2006. In hindsight, Wallace Mercer is a figure so of his time, he seems almost like a caricature. And we can get a good idea of him and his thoughts because he was a huge self-publicist; in a book that he co-wrote in 1988, *Heart to Heart; The Anatomy of a Football Club*, he describes himself as a 'controlled egomaniac' and an 'impresario'. He hosted media shows on both BBC Scotland and Radio Forth (the local Edinburgh radio station) and he had an unusual habit of writing about himself in the third person.

His time as Hearts chairman was hugely successful, resuscitating the club at a time when they were stagnating to a degree barely believable now, and there is no doubt he had a better grasp of the off-field direction of football than many of his contemporaries in Scottish football. A Rangers fan from Glasgow, Hearts under him maintained strong links to Rangers, with Rangers legends Sandy Jardine and Alex MacDonald coming in, and another, Jock Wallace, was courted but refused. His book is sponsored by Scottish Brewers – then a major sponsor of Rangers through McEwan's Lager – and it devotes a bizarre amount of time to talking about Rangers and how successful they were. At one point, Mercer was openly flirting with the possibility of moving to Rangers, 'his first love', to become their chief executive, and he was a shareholder in that club. Later, his plans for a new stadium for Hearts were linked to Rangers owner David Murray's land interests on the west of Edinburgh, the suspicion at the time being that they were trying to use Hearts as the acceptable face of huge development on greenbelt land. A Hibernian historian, Tom Wright, noted that one Edinburgh councillor at the time described them as the 'millionaire casuals wanting to run amok in the green belt'. He let his mask slip when he became frustrated as his attempt got bogged down: 'He hoped that people would see what *Hearts* [emphasis added] were trying to do – make Edinburgh a force in Scottish and European football.' It doesn't take a genius to work out what strips and name the new club would have played under. I think it is not beyond the realms of possibility that Mercer would have tried to tinker with Hearts' traditions at some time in the future, to make them more marketable once they had become this European force, playing at their new stadium, but it certainly was not a proposal to disband Heart of Midlothian FC. If it were, the Hearts would have been protesting with just as much vigour as their Hibernian counterparts, and that simply didn't happen. And while an *Edinburgh Evening News* survey from the time showed that the majority of Hearts supporters didn't support the idea, there was no formal opposition, and the move had the full backing of the Hearts board. Does anyone really think the Hearts board would unanimously back their own club being merged away?

Mercer cited the 'tribalism' he had encountered as one of the reasons he failed, but could this really have come as a surprise to him? He was savvy and had been owner of Hearts for nine years, and in that time he had made a conscious effort to 'take on' and get rid of the hooligan element and the bigotry that some sections of the Hearts support displayed. There was one Hearts match versus

Motherwell when fighting broke out among Hearts and Motherwell fans, and Mercer himself marched over to try and sort it out. He was not some naive newcomer to Scottish or Edinburgh football, wet behind the ears, who didn't understand the nastier side of football supporters. His babe-in-the-woods routine, which only came out afterwards, just doesn't seem to fit the character. And Mercer had written previously about the social, non-monetary value of a football club in 1988 in Heart to Heart: the Anatomy of a Football Club:

> The club [Hearts] has been managed as a social investment ... it is my view that football clubs cannot entirely be run as profit centres. If that was ever to be the case, then important aspects like fellowship and sportsmanship would disappear ... what matters most is the players and the supporters; the business element comes after that.

Rather more ominously, he went on to write:

> In other words, I will use all the business techniques I can and make best use of our situation in Scotland's capital city to help my football club.

Perhaps when we strip away all the PR, all of the revisionism and the media spin, it really was that simple.

An opportunistic takeover of a distressed rival. A simple and commonplace business technique to make *his* football club stronger, remove the competition and make Hearts' self-image complete, as Edina's *only* darlings.

* * *

Just how widespread the opposition was from Hearts supporters is difficult to quantify, particularly in hindsight. The whole episode has not aged well, and Hearts and their fans understandably don't want to be portrayed as predatory, to be the bad guys in the tale. Football fans the world over would recognise what they did as a bad thing, just as fans the world over hated what Milton Keynes Dons did to Wimbledon. The unpalatable reality is that Hearts were the bad guys in this instance, they were predatory, and they did try and shut their greatest rivals down. Did the Hearts support recognise this at the time? There is little evidence of anything; there were no protests, no rallies, no uproar among the Hearts faithful. At the time, there was simply no sense at all that Hearts as a club were in jeopardy, that they were going to disappear; that's just not how it was, no matter how much it is now portrayed as some sort of existential threat to both clubs that they fought off together. The merger, hands across the city stuff, united in anger at the moves of a madman is revisionism.

There were, however, some Hearts fans who stuck their heads above the parapet. John Robertson, the Hammer of Hibs on the pitch, turned up to a Hands Off Hibs rally and showed solidarity with Hibernian. It was a move that earned him a fine from his club (their players had been ordered not to attend), and the respect of Hibernian supporters, despite doing so much damage to them on the pitch over the years.

The takeover was in many ways the logical conclusion of Hearts' identity, particularly on the back of the worst period in Hearts' history. How could Hearts be Edina's Darlings when Hibernian absolutely gained the upper hand for a sustained period? It also fits with the historical view that Hibernian had always been a bit alien, illegitimate, different, not of Edinburgh. As one fan put it when interviewed by academics Kelly & Bairner in 2018:

> For me it [Hearts] was the club that identified with Edinburgh whereas Hibs were in Leith … oh, they're from Leith … so as far as I'm concerned Hearts is Edinburgh's club. Hibs came later. I dunno, maybe it's the Irish connection with Hibs and the roots they came fae' and everything else. I mean Hearts were formed in Edinburgh, Edinburgh people.

And Hearts historian David Speed told them:

> Hearts supporters regard it as 'Edinburgh's club', 'Edina's darlings'. We consider ourselves to be the city's club. I'll come right to the point here, we consider ourselves the superior club.

If, as Mercer and his family have claimed ever since, he won the business argument (whatever that means) that there should only be one club so as not to split resources, then of course that one club would be Hearts, *Edinburgh's* club, the *superior* club. It absolutely fits with Hearts' identity and their sense of their self.

No doubt there would have been Hearts supporters who didn't agree with it or who felt that life without the derby would be less interesting. But there was no concern that Hearts would disappear. And why wouldn't the Hearts fans enjoy seeing their great rivals – who they had absolutely got on top of on the pitch during the 80s – getting trampled underfoot off it?

Perhaps the best measure of the response of Hearts supporters was the derby match that took place after the takeover attempt. It was September after the summer of the takeover, and feelings were running high. There were no displays of contrition, or embarrassment at their club's actions. There was no 'not in our name'. Their fans were celebrating wildly, goading the Hibernian support and revelling in their superiority on and off the park. Robertson, who scored the first, later wrote in his autobiography:

> They [Hibs fans] were hanging over the fences screaming blue murder and wanted their pound of flesh. It was toxic.

Then as he walked back to halfway after scoring the first goal:

I felt a thump on the back of my neck. As I turned round, I was astonished to see it was actually a Hibs fan. Before I could react, Andy Goram [Hibs' goalie] had raced from his goal and pulled the lad away. As that happened, a Hearts fan ran on to the pitch and punched the Hibs fan. Cue bedlam. As the Hearts supporters taunted the home fans, it was too much for some and suddenly the Hibs fans on the east terracing spilled on to the pitch. The teams were taken off while Edinburgh's finest were charged with herding them back.

There were two further, smaller pitch invasions as Hearts raced into a 3-0 half-time lead. At half-time, a police officer entered the Hearts dressing room and told the players that if they scored again, they were worried they wouldn't be able to hold back the Hibernian supporters. The inference being, take your foot off the pedal. Hearts didn't, but neither did they score more as Hibs settled back to damage limitation. The takeover attempt, which Mercer lamented was sunk by tribalism, had increased the tribalism to a level not seen in years, perhaps decades, and there are plenty who think that change was permanent.

Although it might not have seemed like it at the time, better days were ahead for Hibernian, and sooner than anyone dared to dream. In October 1991, just months after they had nearly disappeared, Hibernian faced Dunfermline Athletic in the League Cup Final at Hampden. The greens

THE TEAM THAT WOULDN'T DIE

won a tight match 2-0, and the celebrations could begin. Around 200,000 people were estimated to have come out to see the team return to Edinburgh with an open-top bus parade along Princes St, down Leith Walk and back to Easter Road. It was a remarkable triumph, and one of the few occasions when the gods of football fate seemed to be in charitable mood, recognising that Hibernian fans had gone through something that few, if any, other supports ever have or ever will. They had come out the other end, and got their reward.

There was a lot of karma and irony in Hibernian's triumph. Despite their superiority in the derby through the 80s and their resurgence, Hearts hadn't managed to win a trophy, and had lost a few opportunities in calamitous ways. And just a few months after Hearts tried to buy them over, it was green ribbons on the bus parading along Princes St, bringing Edinburgh to a standstill and taking the acclaim of the city.

As Ian Colquhoun, who wrote a book about this period, noted:

> Hibs' journey from the jaws of death to cup glory was perhaps best summed up by a large home-made banner on the open terracing at Hampden: it simply read 'from oblivion to Hampden'.

Joe Baker has been proved right.

* * *

Mercer may have retired to the South of France after he sold Hearts, but he had one last derby story to be involved in. When he died of cancer in January 2006, as would normally happen Hearts planned to hold a minute's silence, as a mark of respect to their former owner and chairman at their next home match. As football so often does, it created its own narrative, and ensured that Mercer's death would be marked in a perversely appropriate manner; Hearts' next home match was a derby against Hibernian. Of course it was ...

The football media went into overdrive with comment and opinion, sensing the tasty narrative that would fill their previews and reviews of the occasion, and there were many retrospectives on that tumultuous summer. It was an extraordinary time, a move almost unparalleled in modern football history, certainly in the UK. This was something of a bear-trap moment for the Hibernian support, something that many thought Hearts, by choosing to hold what to them was a provocative act, were doing deliberately to embarrass Hibernian, but what club in the world wouldn't honour such an important figure in their history after he had died?

The Hibernian support, which would number around 3,000 at Tynecastle for an Edinburgh Derby, are not always the best embodiment of everything that a club would like its support to portray. They are boisterous, volatile, and usually contain a high percentage of young guys who have spent the hours before the match dampening their inhibitions with all manner of substances. And yet common decency would dictate that a mark of respect for an important figure in the modern history of a club should be honoured.

It was one of those issues where different viewpoints quickly became partisan, and only those who wilfully wanted the occasion to be used to make a point failed to grasp the genuine complexities of honouring this man, at this time. This was not business as usual, and Wallace Mercer was not some benign or even anonymous club blazer who had faithfully worked away in the background of a rival club.

To Hearts fans, he was the architect of the modern club. His chairmanship saw Hearts emerge from the doldrums. He was a moderniser, especially by the standards of the staid and conventional world of Scottish football, where 'small c' conservatism was regularly seen as a virtue. Like him or loathe him, and plenty of Hearts fans were heading towards the latter by the end of his period of ownership, he was impossible to ignore, and he made a serious and lasting impression on Hearts, and on Scottish football in general.

To Hibernian fans Mercer was, and still is, the devil incarnate. He was the man who, with no emotion, sense of morality or regard for 115 years of social and sporting history, attempted to kill their club and wipe it from the footballing map, all to give his club a better chance of success. What's more, he never showed any sense of contrition or regret for his actions, just as he showed no empathy whatsoever towards Hibernian or its supporters. He approached his task with a surgical calmness that betrayed the fact he just didn't care about the effects of his actions. To Hibernian supporters and many neutral observers, this displayed a callousness and lack of morality that was hard to fathom, and even harder to defend. Fans of any club can understand the Hibernian supporters' anger; after all, how would any support react if, when faced with severe financial difficulties, their closest rivals made a predatory and opportunistic attempt to take them over and erase them from football?

Mercer remains unforgiven by the green half of Edinburgh, and to this day Hibernian fans sing derogatory and distasteful songs about him. They do not see wallowing in the death of a fellow human being as something indecent; instead they approach the subject with the same disregard of decency and morality as he approached their club. As Mercer himself put it, tribalism won. Most of the Hibernian support turned their backs on the minute's silence, plenty sang, held their scarves, goaded their Hearts rivals and generally tried to disrupt it. Hearts won the match, in a way that was fitting to their derby record under Mercer. But Hibernian were still there, which was the victory that the Hibernian fans had fought for.

CHAPTER 15

TIME OF CHANGE

1991–1998

THE 1990s was a decade in which everything changed in football, a decade that began in one era – the era of terracing, crowd sways and violence, and ended in the gilded age of the English Premier League, new stadiums and the Bosman ruling. Stadium building work in particular was a perennial of the 90s, in response to the Hillsborough disaster.

The new rules requiring all-seater grounds following Hillsborough put a huge financial strain on clubs, with very few being able to just build new stadiums in one go. Instead, the odd new stand would appear, towering above the old remaining terraces, which were in turn seated, creating shallow banks of seated enclosures meaning most clubs' capacities were reduced, and lots of people got very wet sitting in uncovered seats. At Easter Road they seated the away end, before building two large modern stands behind either goal, but left in place the old main stand and the old terracing down either touchline. At Tynecastle, they had a large uncovered bank of seats at one end (the old Gorgie

Road terracing), and demolished the other end behind the goals, leaving a blank space. The main stand remained, and opposite stood a single enormous new stand, made to look even bigger by it standing on its own, although the School End stand was soon to follow. This meant that Tynecastle was literally half redeveloped, giving it a very lopsided feel. The same happened across the country, where Celtic had a single, enormous stand and nothing behind either goal, and Aberdeen and Motherwell[54] both built huge single stands behind one goal that dwarfed the rest of the ground, making them look very lopsided, a state in which both grounds remain to this day, 30 years later. And while the state and design of stadiums remained a source of argument between the fans, it has to be said that the Edinburgh Derby is much better for both clubs still being at their traditional homes, and that both clubs have done a good job of creating modern facilities on the old footprint, the restraints of the sites giving the grounds a bespoke feel that perfect, symmetrical, purpose-built grounds on empty land struggle to recreate.

In 1991, Hibernian FC achieved a historic victory in the League Cup, coming from the brink of financial ruin to an unlikely triumph. It was one of the greatest victories in Hibernian's history, and 'the team that wouldn't die' went down in club folklore. Fittingly, the two main players that day were both local lads and Hibernian fans, who must have felt the strain of the takeover attempt more than most: Micky Weir, who was man of the match and won the penalty for their first goal, and Keith Wright, whose clinching second goal in the final meant he had scored in every round.

That League Cup win was huge for Hibernian, and the celebration in Edinburgh afterwards went long into the night: part-celebration, part-release of pent-up emotions – a perfect response after the takeover attempt and the financial troubles they had got themselves into. And when Hibernian reached the League Cup Final again in 1993, their fans might have been forgiven for thinking that the new decade would bring new opportunities, but Rangers beat them 2-1 in the second final, and familiar failings would remain. They were making little headway in the league to begin with, finishing second bottom in 1990/91 as they recovered from their financial difficulties and hostile takeover attempt by Hearts, before getting safely into mid-table. They then managed a run of fifth, third, fifth, building up what had the makings of a decent team, but it all unravelled very quickly indeed, and a team that finished second bottom – having to win a relegation play-off against Airdrieonians to stay up, relying heavily on star players goalkeeper Jim Leighton and forward Darren Jackson – then lost Leighton on a Bosman and sold Jackson to Celtic. What happens when you take the two best players out of a team that finished second bottom? That's right, they finished bottom, and Hibernian were relegated in season 1997/98, although they did bounce straight back, winning the second tier in season 1998/99.

For most of the 1990s Hearts were competitive, and from the mid-90s onwards there was a definite sense that they were building towards something. A couple of managerial false starts in the early years meant that mid-table finishes came either side of an impressive second place in 1991/92. Three more years of mid-table mediocrity followed as Jim Jefferies, recruited from Falkirk, started to build a very capable side. Their main quest lay in trying to end their trophy drought. Since Hibernian had won the League Cup in 1991, they had been mercilessly taunting their rivals about their lack of trophies. Hearts were getting closer, reaching three Scottish Cup semi-finals in four seasons, although their old failings at that round kept resurfacing. In two of those years, both Hibernian and Hearts were in the semi-finals, but on both occasions both sides lost, to mean there would be no all-Edinburgh final.

Hearts did eventually get over the hurdle, and they made the 1996 cup final, losing 5-1 to Rangers, and the next season they lost the League Cup Final to Rangers 4-3 in a thrilling match. Hearts had lost again but they were gearing up, and in season 1997/98 they sprung. A title challenge materialised that lasted most of the year before petering out into a still credible third-place finish, but it was in the Scottish Cup Final that this season would be defined. They played Rangers at Celtic Park, and took an amazing early lead through a penalty in the second minute. The match was tight, until early in the second half Hearts made it two. Then it became like the Alamo, as Rangers threw everything at Hearts, even managing to pull one back with nine minutes remaining. But Hearts held firm, winning their first trophy in 36 years. It was, in the eyes of every Hearts fan I spoke to, the greatest moment of their football lives, lifting a huge burden of near misses that had been weighing heavily on the club for decades. Hearts suffered a bit of a hangover the next year, struggling in a relegation battle before eventually finishing sixth, but they didn't care, their job had been done.

The other defining feature of the 1990s was, of course, the derby. Having commenced their unbeaten run in the 80s, it ran into the 90s for Hearts; it would, astonishingly, continue until April 1994, when Hibernian eventually won 1-0 at Tynecastle.

Tony moved to Edinburgh in early 1991 as a ten-year-old. Not being from Scotland and having no family influence to push him to support one club or another, he initially took a liking to Aberdeen, with Eoin Jess his favourite player.[55] But as he went to high school, and became a veteran of Edinburgh juvenile football, he got sucked into the Edinburgh rivalry. 'I had friends who were fans of both clubs, so I went to see them both quite regularly, they were always trying to convert me! I suppose I was quite unique, in that I am a massive football fan, but I never had a team to support – I'm as close to a genuine neutral football fanatic as you can get.'

'It's an intense rivalry,' he tells me of his time immersed in Edinburgh. 'I would say on a par with the Old Firm – although obviously on a smaller scale – which might surprise outsiders.' He uses the term 'outsiders', because as far as he is concerned Edinburgh is his home town, where he spent his formative years, and with whose accent he still speaks, despite being in London for a decade. He tells me that some of his mates started going on a particular Hearts supporters' bus where anti-Catholic songs and language were commonplace, and they started getting involved in that too, despite not really understanding it. I ask him if it caused problems among his wider group of mates?

'Sometimes it did. There were more Jambos in our group at school, it was a very Hearts school, and though we were a big group of mates, it used to flare up from time to time. There were definitely individuals within the group who were never very close, and football was a big part of the reason for that – there was always just a wee edge between them. Interestingly, they tended to be the ones whose families were steeped in the rivalry, rather than those who had just picked a team (Hearts in this case) to go along with the majority. The Hibbies had a tough time, not just because they were hugely outnumbered at my school, but also because Hearts really had the upper hand on the pitch.'

The period Tony refers to was the end of the 22-games-in-a-row period, Hearts' record unbeaten run in the fixture. And while Hibernian managed to break that run in 1994 and secure some victories of their own, Hearts moved quickly into the successful Jim Jefferies era, building an exciting team who once again held the advantage over their rivals as they slid towards relegation. Tony continues, 'In that era Hearts were the much more successful team, especially with derby matches. They were more direct, ruthless and ultimately effective. Hibs though were the more likeable, an underdog who could be romanticised.

They always seemed to play the better football. Looking back, there were times where I was convinced Hibs were better but Hearts always won. It seemed the script was Hibs would play all the football but Hearts would win with a deflected shot in the 80th minute, or something like that. That's how I remember it, anyway.'

His memory isn't completely playing tricks on him. Just as Hearts' derby record in the 80s was built on their ability to win tight matches, so it continued into the 90s. Between August 1991 (a 0-0 draw) and Hearts' 22nd undefeated match (also a 0-0), there was never more than three goals in a match, and only once was there more than one goal between the teams, a 2-0 victory in 1993. Even when Hibernian broke the sequence and won two successive matches, they were 1-0 and 2-1. Hearts' ability to somehow win or at least not lose tight derby matches was incredible. The 1990s saw a lot of change in football, but some things stayed constant.

CHAPTER 16

MONEY'S TOO TIGHT
TO MENTION

1999–2012

THE POST-BOSMAN, hyper-monied era of football has made it even more difficult for clubs like Hearts and Hibernian to build on success. Football at this level is much more short-term than it used to be; good players are sold (as they ever were), but now good players are sold more quickly to capitalise on values before contracts start running down, young players are often signed as teenagers before they even play, and large swathes of the first teams are made up of one- or two-year contracts, and increasingly loans, as those young players hoovered up by the super-clubs need game time to develop, after all. The turn of the millennium was when this really started to become apparent, and it had an impact on the way the derby has developed. Long periods of domination like we saw in the 1970s for Hibernian, or the 80s/90s for Hearts, are now much less common. So it was that just as Hearts seemed to be building towards something, the tables quickly turned.

Hibernian won promotion at a canter, and they brought that momentum back up into the Premier League with them. Led by the brilliant Franck Sauzee and Russell Latapy, Hibernian consolidated comfortably back in the league, and looked to be building something. Hearts were trying to build, using their new-found wealth to sign a raft of players, a significant outlay for a club of their size. But the first sign that things were not going well came in the traditional new year derby, which took place at Tynecastle in December 1999, the 'millennium derby'. Hibernian were surprisingly dominant, and Hearts just couldn't get going. The visitors were already a goal up when Franck Sauzee rifled in a second from outside the box, and they rounded off a surprise 3-0 win late in the match. Hibernian followed this victory up, and Franck Sauzee secured his legacy, when he lost his two front teeth scoring a header in a 3-1 win at Easter Road.

The next season was a vintage one for Hibernian as they mixed it with the Old Firm for the first half of the season. While their form did tail off after Christmas, they had third place wrapped up very early, and could concentrate on getting to the final of the Scottish Cup, where they lost, again, to Celtic, again, by 3-0. The highlight of that season came the previous October, when Hearts travelled across town to Easter Road on a Sunday evening. Hibernian tore their rivals apart, winning 6-2 in what was one of the greatest performances a Hibernian team had ever put in at Easter Road. The 6-2 result remains iconic for Hibernian supporters, both because of the result but also the style in which they played. There was one last hurrah for this Hibernian side in the following season's UEFA Cup. Drawn to play AEK Athens, Hibernian lost the first leg in Athens 2-0 (in a match that was delayed for a week due to the September 11 attacks). In an echo of the glorious European nights of old, Hibernian roared back in the second leg at Easter Road, winning 2-0 and taking the match to extra time (they were also within a whisker of scoring a third in the last minute of normal time to win the tie). For Hibernian supporters, that night is iconic, and many will say it was the best atmosphere they ever experienced at Easter Road; if not ever, then at least since the ground was reduced in size in the 1980s. It was also the night (ironically) that the fans first sang 'Sunshine on Leith', which was belted out at the end of normal time. AEK pooped the party, by scoring two goals quickly in extra time (and away goals always had an especially deflating effect on home crowds in Europe), and while Hibernian came back to win the match 3-2, they went out on aggregate 4-3. In hindsight, 'Sunshine on Leith' was a lament for this era.

For Hearts fans it was a sobering period. From looking like they were about to establish dominance, Hibernian had turned the tables on them. For Jim Jefferies, a legendary Hearts figure, it was tough to bear. He had played in the 0-7 match in 1973, and now here he was as manager suffering the biggest defeat since.

Jefferies was sacked and Hearts appointed Craig Levein to take over. Levein had been a classy central defender at

Hearts in the 1980s, and only injury prevented him from progressing to England. Importantly for Hearts supporters, despite his managerial inexperience he had been part of the Hearts team that had dominated Hibernian in the 80s and 90s, with an impressive record. While he didn't achieve quite that level of dominance as manager, he certainly upended Hibernian's recent success, and got Hearts back up towards the top of the table. Off the pitch, his time was marked by disruption as angry Hearts supporters fought with their ownership – something that he very successfully prevented from impacting the team – and where his time was marked by consistency, and some legendary derby results.

Perhaps the most famous was the 5-1 match (not that one, the first one), although in truth the 5-1 score is slightly misleading, as the match was 2-1 until the second half, when Hearts sealed the win with a third. In what was both a trademark of Levein's first spell as manager, and an enormous psychological hurdle for Hibernian at this time (not just against Hearts, their record of conceding late goals became a phenomenon), they conceded late goals, two on this occasion, to give a thumping scoreline and leave Hibernian punch-drunk. It was a trick they were to repeat in the next two derby matches. Trailing by 1-0 at Easter Road with just six minutes left, Hearts hit a classic 1-2 to steal a late – and brilliantly undeserved – win in injury time. Then in the next match, Hibernian were winning 3-2 as the match entered injury time. They then got a penalty which they missed but scored the rebound from to make it 4-2 and seal the victory. Until a young striker – never heard of before or since, Graeme Weir – astonishingly scored two goals in injury time to level the match 4-4. It was an incredible sequence of results for Hearts, and Levein seemed to have brought that X factor from the derbies of his playing days.

It was around this time that both clubs' off-field difficulties started, and Hibernian's cost-cutting started to have a real impact on the pitch, with them finishing tenth, seventh and eighth in the league. It was also around this time that Hibernian announced they were considering proposals to sell Easter Road, and move to a new stadium at Straiton, just outside the city boundaries to the south (in Midlothian, ironically enough) on undeveloped land owned by Tom Farmer, their owner. This was not a popular proposal for supporters, and that was before it was revealed that the two clubs were in discussions to share the new ground, as part of Hearts' plans to sell Tynecastle to address their own levels of debt. The Hibernian supporters made it very clear from the start that this was out of the question for them. The negative associations of a new, 'flatpack stadium' weren't helped by the land at Straiton being just beside the huge Ikea store; the headlines wrote themselves.

Both sets of fans were up in arms – Hearts supporters moving to a new part of town to help the owner of Hibernian make money from empty land; Hibernian supporters for helping Hearts out of a hole of their own making. And that was without the unpalatable prospect to both sides of sharing their home with the other lot. It may have made short-term financial sense, but it definitely didn't make football sense to either club.

At the time, the boards of both clubs could point to their duty to explore all options, and to ensure the futures of the clubs, and their levels of debt were extraordinary for clubs of their size. But in hindsight, leaving aside the rights and wrongs and financial arguments, it is impossible not to think that Edinburgh football would have been a far duller, less interesting proposition if both clubs had left their historic homes, in their historic districts, and moved to a new stadium in the middle of nowhere. The whole experience of going to matches at either ground would be transformed, and ripping both clubs from their communities, from their little patches of green boxed in by tenements and roads, such as they are, would have stripped the rivalry of so much of its identity.

It is at this point that there is a clear break in the road between the two clubs; an inflection point that has gone a long way to shaping the rivalry ever since. Because both clubs were in very similar positions, for very similar reasons, and despite looking at the same solution (and even sharing a solution), the club's approaches diverged, and then some. Hibernian, in the face of a furious reaction by their supporters to the proposed Straiton project, relented and implemented a new plan. They would stay at Easter Road, as long as the fans backed them to the tune of hitting average crowds of 11,000, which they had identified as a new break-even point. This break-even point was tough, and would involve swingeing cuts, cuts that saw great servants on the pitch discarded, quite callously (John O'Neil for example, who they stopped playing, allegedly for financial reasons related to his contract). The Hibernian board sold their fans a reality of facing the consequences of overspending, and their refusal to countenance moving from their Holy Ground – you can stay at Easter Road, but you are going to have to pay for it.

The path chosen by Hearts was in stark contrast to the prosaic one offered by the Hibernian board. The Hearts fans continued to hound out their board, and so they sold out, and sent the club down a very different path.

Hearts, under Levein, managed consecutive third-place finishes, and some notable results in Europe, playing a very physical, very defensive style. It was a style that would dog Levein's time as Scotland manager a few years later, but it definitely worked for Hearts.

A happy side-effect from Hibernian's drastic cost-cutting was that they discovered they had a vintage group of youth players, all of whom were quickly established in the team. And under new manager Tony Mowbray, a style of football was introduced to Easter Road that made the most of the talents and they finished third, fourth and sixth in the next three seasons, the last of which, 2006/07, saw them win the League Cup with a brilliant 5-1 victory over Kilmarnock in the final. Hibernian then stagnated badly as the young talent was sold, to continue getting rid of the debt and invest in infrastructure – a new stand (to complete the redevelopment of the ground) and a brand-new training centre. The next three seasons saw Hibernian finish sixth,

sixth and fourth, before they plummeted into relegation fights in seasons 2010/11 and 2011/12 as years of eroding the football side finally started to tell.

Hearts on the other hand were entering the Vladimir Romanov years. They finished fifth in season 2004/05 under legend John Robertson. They also got to both cup semi-finals, losing the League Cup semi to Motherwell. Despite scoring two goals in the last five minutes to take the match to extra time, they conceded the winner in the last minute of extra time. They lost to Celtic in the Scottish Cup semi-final. Season 2005/06 was when the Romanov era really began in earnest, with a blistering start under George Burley, they went 13 matches unbeaten before losing the derby to Hibernian at Easter Road, although they did hammer Hibernian three times that season, including 4-0 in the Scottish Cup semi-final on the way to winning it against Gretna in the final. The Romanov era didn't really deliver on the pitch though, and fourth-, eighth- and third-place finishes in the following seasons were a poor return for the money being spent. They also lost to Hibernian in the League Cup quarter-finals at Easter Road as their rivals went on to clinch the trophy. A sixth- and third-place finish followed, before a fifth-place finish in season 2011/12. But nobody remembers where Hearts finished in the league that season, and nobody cares.

A poor Hibernian side, who finished second bottom of the league somehow, made it to the Scottish Cup Final where they would face Hearts, for the first time since 1896. It was a match fraught with risk and loaded with potential reward. For Hearts, it was the chance to win another cup under Romanov by beating their greatest rivals. For Hibernian, the chance to end the curse against Hearts. It was written in the stars!

Hearts hammered Hibernian on the day, winning 5-1. They were undoubtedly aided by two big refereeing decisions that went their way – VAR might have had a big impact on the match – but that wasn't why Hibernian lost. Hearts raced into a two-goal lead, although Hibs pulled one back just before half-time to give the match a different complexion. Then, just after half-time, Hibernian's hapless left-back pulled down Hearts' winger outside the box. He received a second booking, and a penalty was given; at 3-1 v ten men, it was game over. Hearts eventually won 5-1, and they weren't exactly going hell for leather by the end. It was quite simply the greatest derby victory in living memory, and one of the greatest ever. They had humiliated their rivals and, as a bonus, extended their barren run in the Scottish Cup.

It was a dreadful Hibernian performance, from a dreadful Hibernian team, full of short-term contracts and loanees from England. It was exactly what it was; a crap Hibernian team who finished second bottom of the league. In hindsight, it would have been a cruel irony if that motley crew had managed to do what so many great players in the past had been unable to. But nobody in green would have complained, obviously. It was a colossal blow to take, and for a while everyone at the club was punch-drunk. After a defeat like that in the last game of the season, the fans are demanding answers, statements, resignations – anything to show something was happening. They got none of that; instead they got a summer of ridicule and worry. For Hearts fans, it was a vindication of the Romanov era. They had put Hibernian firmly in their place, it was a victory to top even that of 1998, and they, and hundreds of thousands of the people of Edinburgh, celebrated with the traditional open-top bus parade.

There must have been a lot of Hibernian fans hiding in their beds that Sunday, nursing terrible hangovers and bad doses of *the fear*.

CHAPTER 17

BOOM AND BUST

'Vladimir gave me this dismissive flick of the
hand as if to say Hibs aren't our rivals. He
never thought they were. He thought we were
challenging Rangers and Celtic.'

– Phil Hay, The Athletic

IT'S IRONIC that Vladimir Romanov didn't think
Hibernian were his rivals, because his ownership has ended
up being defined by, and helping to define, the Edinburgh
Derby more than any other event since the attempted
takeover in 1990. His time in charge of Hearts remains
enigmatic, and chatting to Hearts supporters there remains
a sense of residual conflict in how they view it; they know
he was mad and, more than that, he was malign, and he
– willingly assisted by an army of enablers – very nearly
ruined Hearts. On the flipside, would *that* cup final have
happened without him? And if not, how could you hate the
guy that made that possible?

* * *

Hearts and Romanov were a match made in heaven. The Russian/Lithuanian, a former Soviet submarine captain whose wealth was of unknown origin, had apparently been rebuffed by three Scottish clubs already – Dunfermline Athletic, Dundee and Dundee United – which should have served as a warning. The lack of a credible backstory, the lack of an obvious source for his wealth, the fact the bank he owned was just the fifth-biggest in Lithuania – small fry in global banking – and was trying to break into the Edinburgh financial sector should have set alarm bells ringing.[56] But at that time Hearts had got used to the sounds of alarm bells. In fact, alarm bells had been ringing at Tynecastle non-stop for some time, to the point that I'm not sure anyone noticed them anymore. All they saw, all they cared about was that here was someone who apparently had wealth that he was willing to throw at Hearts. As George Foulkes, the Hearts chairman at the time, said, 'I brought him in because he was going to put some money in.'

Foulkes had taken Romanov around Westminster as his guest in an attempt to court his interest, and had his background 'checked'. Craig Watson, who wrote about this period in Hearts' history, tells us that 'the politician went as far as to urge other major shareholders to be realistic about the price they could expect to get for their stake in their club'. Foulkes describing Romanov as a 'white knight' was acting as his cheerleader, to the point that some Hearts fans even complained to the Financial Services Authority about his actions affecting the share price.

At the start of 2004, *The Independent* newspaper reported that Motherwell, Livingston, Dundee and Dunfermline Athletic were all in severe financial troubles, and Rangers and Kilmarnock were starting to hit difficulties. In Edinburgh, the report went on, Hibernian were embarking on a huge cost-cutting exercise – including putting their manager on notice in order to force him to accept a new contract on a lower salary – and selling off anything not nailed down to reduce their own £14.5m debt. Hearts' debt was at £17.6m. Hearts were, in business parlance, a distressed asset. They were drowning in debt, and to resolve this their Tynecastle Park home had been sold to housing developers. The club were in open civil war as a result, with a huge fans' movement starting up to campaign to keep Hearts at Tynecastle and force current owner, the deeply unpopular Chris Robinson, out of the club. Romanov looked like the answer to their prayers, and given their perilous situation you can't blame Hearts fans for embracing this apparently kind stranger; and boy did he give them plenty to embrace. He immediately won the fans over with talk of usurping the Old Firm, even winning the Champions League (to general and widespread howls of derision), all through spending millions of his own money, making Hearts debt-free and saving Tynecastle. To his credit, he did achieve the last of those promises.

This was not long after Roman Abramovich, another hitherto unknown Russian, had appeared out of nowhere to rescue a heavily indebted football club, then lavished unlimited wealth upon it out of the goodness of his heart.

Hearts thought they had found their version of Abramovich, and Romanov had his cheerleaders in Edinburgh that helped him foster this image. According to Watson, 'Foulkes was discussing the possibility that the club could "find a foreign backer, as Chelsea did".' Hearts fans were desperate to buy what Romanov was selling. They were in a bad way, facing enormous financial problems and he was savvy enough to tell Hearts supporters what they wanted to hear.

He tapped into their long-held beliefs and to their very identity; he told them they were the premier club in Edinburgh, that he would take on and challenge the Old Firm, and lift Hearts to another level, that Hibernian were no longer their rivals, and he would do all of this out of generosity, and to promote his bank in some unspecified way. For Hearts fans this was manna from heaven. Not only would they not have to suffer the indignity of the harsh financial realities they found themselves in, they would get to spend their way out of trouble and fulfil what they see as their destiny to become Scotland's third-most successful club.

Romanov firstly cancelled the sale of Tynecastle Park and transferred their debt to his own previously unheard-of bank, Ukio. He also bought a grand – and incredibly expensive – old bank building in the centre of Edinburgh which he proclaimed would become the new headquarters of said bank. On the field, Hearts flirted very publicly in the media with a host of high-profile managers, most notably Bobby Robson. And while that never came off, George Burley, who had done a brilliant job at Ipswich

Town in the English Premiership, was brought in and represented something of a coup. Burley was quickly joined by a host of players from across Europe (as well as a load from Lithuania), and the plan looked like coming off. Hearts started that season in incredible form, with eight straight wins, and 13 matches unbeaten, including against Rangers as well as a 4-0 hammering of Hibernian. They were top of the league, and looked like they could mount a genuine title challenge. Then out of the blue, Romanov sacked George Burley. And just as the Hearts support took up their new anthem, 'We are unbeatable', after 13 matches without defeat they went to Easter Road and Hibernian defeated them, winning a tense match 2-0.

Hearts didn't buckle though, and although the title challenge fell away gradually, they finished the season strongly enough to claim second place, and a tilt at qualifying for the Champions League. They also hammered Hibernian 4-0 (again) in the Scottish Cup semi-final to book a place against third-tier Gretna (basically a non-league club who had been inflated through financial doping, and went bust shortly afterwards). Hearts got a shock in the final, but eventually won on penalties. It was the first trophy under Romanov, to go with a second-place finish. At this point, it seemed Hearts were on the brink of something special, like they were really going to achieve another golden era and win lots of trophies. But the rest of his reign descended into a chaotic lurching from brilliant to barmy at regular intervals, and all the while, the doubts and questions about his dubious money were swept away;

out of sight, out of mind. As sports writer Phil Hay put it in The Athletic: 'The 2005–06 season would encapsulate the contradiction of Romanov; his knack of giving Hearts memories to treasure while simultaneously taking them to the brink of collapse. The whole point of it, and this worked well, was that we wanted to own Edinburgh, to take total ownership of the city in a football sense.'

Romanov spent a lot of time coming across as an idiot, making daft comments in the media, courting controversy. But Romanov was nobody's fool. He hired a global PR firm to act as his spokesperson and media advisers. He railed against the injustice of Scottish football, how the Scottish football media and the Old Firm conspired to keep Hearts down, at the same time as he employed former BBC Scotland football commentator and reporter, Charlie Mann, as his spokesman, and his club PR team also included a former reporter from the *Edinburgh Evening News*. The Romanov era is a strange one to look back on and judge. On the one hand it delivered a Champions League qualifying round, and two Scottish Cups, one a nerve-jangling penalty shoot-out win over third-tier Gretna; the other Hearts' greatest ever result, the 5-1 hammering of Hibernian. But he also took Hearts to the very brink, duped the supporters, brought ridicule on their club and, of course, left financial wreckage behind him affecting thousands of others. He has never spoken of his time, and according to newspaper reports from Lithuania, he fled that country and returned to Russia to escape the consequences of his financial impropriety. Ian Murray, one of the politicians who helped to drive forward the rescue attempt, summed it up: 'Many supporters will have a marmite attitude to Vladimir Romanov. I think it would be unfair to label him as some sort of pariah. It is worth remembering that, despite his obvious eccentricities, he did deliver some of the most memorable moments in the history of the club.'

'So what did, and do, the actual Hearts supporters make of Romanov in his years in charge?' I asked my mate Neil, a Hearts fan who is in his 40s now and so lived through the whole episode. 'Christ, you could write a trilogy on that madman. I have strange feelings towards him. He caused utter carnage and was a fucking wanker for most of the time, but he gave us hope, even if it was fleeting.'

As we see with many clubs across the UK, football fans will excuse almost anything if it brings them on-field success. For Hearts fans, the endless musical chairs with managers and players are easily forgiven, as they would be for any set of fans. The ridicule he brought upon the club, likewise, is easily forgotten; many Hearts fans can look back on that period and have a laugh at Mad Vlad and his antics. The financial ruin he left behind is very much out of sight, out of mind, as most of it affected people in Lithuania. But what of that enormous list of creditors who had to involuntarily lose money for Hearts to succeed? Hearts fans tend to brush off difficult questions like that, and either downplay it or point to another club who did similarly, neither of which answer the question. The Romanov era ended in an historic, famous victory for them over Hibernian, and for many that was worth any cost, short of the club dying.

At a derby match around that time Hibernian fans held up a banner that read 'we paid for your poppies, lest you forget'. The banner was swiftly removed by stewards (despite the match being at Easter Road). As always with football rivalry, there are no absolute truths and every story has at least two sides. Hibernian supporters point out that the famous victory at Hampden was when Hearts were living off money they owed to others (and actually not paying the players' wages), and those others – including the NHS, the Lady Haig Poppy Factory, and Hearts' own club charity, not to mention hundreds of other creditors – paid for that triumph without consent or contrition. For a club so closely associated with the noble sacrifice of ordinary men in World War One, it is a difficult truth to face, that the charity which works to commemorate the fallen of World War One should be left out of pocket by Hearts. We have seen how central the military sacrifice of Hearts in the Great War is to the club, and of course that's why the Hibernian supporters chose those words.

But equally, the Hearts fans were relatively powerless in the games that those with wealth played out above their heads. It is a horrible thing about being a football supporter, when you have almost zero control over an institution that you love. They probably could have shown more humility or contrition, and perhaps not been quite as fawning, singing his name, wearing Russian hats, but, ultimately, they were at the whims of an unpredictable and dangerous man who didn't care about the club the way they did. If the fans had turned on Romanov, you have to imagine that Romanov would have turned on the fans, and then maybe it wouldn't have turned out as well as it did in the end.

It is also hard to draw direct lines between events and how things might have worked out differently now. Hearts had agreed the sale of Tynecastle to pay their debts when Romanov took over. Losing Tynecastle wouldn't have killed Hearts like some of the more extreme predictions at the time claimed – Hearts were, and are, too big to fail in Scottish football, and would have been resuscitated and worked their way back, just as Rangers did after they were liquidated – but the club would have still lost a lot. And from a neutral's point of view, Scottish football would be a duller, less interesting place if shorn of one of its great traditional venues. Hearts would have emerged debt-free from that sale, but they would have been homeless. Critics could say that would be fair; after all, Hearts benefitted from spending all of that money that they couldn't pay back, and many other clubs suffered in order to trade their way out of debt. Hearts did emerge from the Romanov era debt-free – albeit by walking away from the debt, rather than paying it – kept Tynecastle, and due to the benevolence of Ann Budge and others, and the commitment of their fans, emerged from administration, first into Budge's ownership and subsequently into supporter ownership.

I found this chapter one of the more difficult to approach, because it is very recent history. Assessing the rights and wrongs of things that happened decades ago is more straightforward and usually less emotive. But everyone around today lived through this era, they revelled in the 5-1 cup final, they suffered through the administration and the worry that the club would lose Tynecastle or even be wound up completely (which seemed a real possibility). It is hard to get perspective on such recent events, and it is hard to even ask questions of Hearts and Hibernian supporters about this era without getting very emotional and defensive responses. For Hearts supporters, it is difficult to untangle the excesses of Romanov from the positive outcome that they ended up with.

It is definitely a quirk that this era in Hearts history should have interacted, impacted and contrasted with their city rivals quite as much as it did. Hearts could just as easily have played Aberdeen in that 2012 cup final, and while it would have still been great for them to win it, it wouldn't be quite as special, quite so historic. And perhaps Hibernian fans wouldn't feel quite so personally affected by the financial doping of the Romanov years. That Hibernian should be one of the teams penalised most by those years is a brilliant perversity of the football gods. Hearts fans love that, Hibernian fans hate it.

Both Hibernian and Hearts entered the Romanov era in similar levels of debt. Yet Hibs chose to pay it back, cut their spending on their squad, and suffered as a result. And when, through necessity, they discovered they had a team of brilliant young players, they watched them all leave, sold off to pay debts, pay for the reconstruction of Easter Road, and buy and fit out their own training ground.

Hearts continued to spend on players, agreed a long-term lease from a nearby university (who, as it turned out, didn't receive a big chunk of that rent and were another on the list of creditors who lost money), lived on the never-never, then rubbed it in their faces when their team triumphed *directly against them*. How could that not annoy them, how could that not affect the rivalry?

From a Hibernian point of view, Hearts had been spending more money than they had since the late 1980s under Mercer, and rather than address that they just kept kicking the can down the road, until such times as the debt became unmanageable. Their critical view is that Hearts were too arrogant and self-important to take the hit on the field, and exist at a more sustainable level. As one Hibernian fan put it to me, 'Hearts want to be the top team in Edinburgh and third force in Scotland, and they don't care how much of other people's money they use to do it.' It's in situations like this that intangibles, like identity, become important. Perhaps if Hearts didn't have so much riding on being the top club in Edinburgh, and becoming the third-best team in Scotland, they might have simply bitten the bullet and started to live within their means. But they had become addicted to the money, and after that taste of success in 1998 they were desperate for more. Going 42 years without a trophy while their great rivals won two must have been painful, and not something they wanted to repeat. As with everything else in this rich rivalry, it will be argued about, and fought over, and eventually become just another part of the story.

And while football creates amazing stories, it also has a brilliant capacity to strip them away and reveal simple facts; matches won, and matches lost, etc. Hearts ended the Romanov era with two Scottish Cup victories, both won at the direct expense of Hibernian with thumping victories at Hampden in the semi-final and final respectively. They were relegated in 2014, after receiving a points penalty for their administration, the final admission that they were never going to pay back the money they had spent. That Hibernian conspired to join them in that relegation after a calamitous end to the season is another story, but certainly softened the blow. Not only did Hibernian suffer more than most from the financial doping, they managed to make sure they suffered the same punishment as Hearts! But Hibs fans would also point out that Hibernian have won the same number of trophies as Hearts since Romanov took over, and they didn't waste millions of other people's money to do it. Although they both took very different routes, they ultimately ended up in the same destination; two cups in the trophy cabinet, and a humiliating relegation each.

When I was speaking to my friend Neil about Romanov, he summed it up nicely: 'The start was great, the middle was meh, and the end was horrible barring the 5-1. It led to clearing our debt and getting fan ownership.'

The Romanov era continues to cast a long shadow across the Edinburgh Derby. When both clubs faced that inflection point around selling their grounds and paying their debts their paths diverged, although ironically it set them on a collision course. Hearts' successes in the Scottish

Cup seemed to elevate their own sense of themselves. Gone were the plucky Hearts who would conspire to lose, the 'always the bridesmaid'[57] Hearts, the Hearts who almost went part-time in the early 80s due to their yo-yo years. Instead, this was 'big team' Hearts, who cared about winning the Scottish Cup, not just for its own sake – and as good as it was, particularly the 1998 victory – but because it reinforced Hibernian's dismal run in the tournament; and in turn it strengthens Hearts' identity as the 'big team' in Edinburgh, a new moniker that has been popularised by the rise of internet chat and fan culture. Hibernian are obviously the 'wee team'. Hearts had left their historic rivals trailing by demonstrating their on-field superiority in both the 2006 and the 2012 Scottish Cup victories. And not only that; not only had they won, they had stopped Hibernian from winning and so helped to extend their long Scottish Cup curse.

The Romanov years allowed Hearts to live the literal manifestation of 130-odd years of struggle and rivalry; the attempt to have Hibernian expelled from football in the 1880s; breaking the rules on professionalism to try and beat Hibernian in the cup in the same era; trying to buy Hibernian over in 1990 and literally wipe them from the map – for Hearts and their supporters Romanov was helping them to achieve what they had been trying to achieve ever since that Edinburgh Cup Final of 1878; Romanov delivered that to them. Or the hundreds of people who lost tens, possibly hundreds, of millions of pounds delivered that to them; like I said, that argument will never really end.

There is still much disputed territory within the story, and the period remains enigmatic, but what is beyond doubt is that the heroes of the story did act with courage and passion to save their club from financial ruin, regardless of how they came to end up in that situation. And there were many, many heroes. High-profile individuals played an important part in galvanising and leading, but it was the 8,000 Hearts supporters who, en masse, backed their club with the necessary funds to keep them going and ultimately help them return to the top of Scottish football. They say that all is well that ends well, and that has proven to be the case for Hearts and their supporters.

There is an irony that the man who was so dismissive of Hibernian as rivals would do so much to shape the rivalry and that his legacy would utterly depend on it. If it wasn't for those moments against Hibernian, the assessment of Romanov's time would be very different among Hearts fans. Hearts spent tens of millions, possibly more than £100 million, during Romanov's tenure, and made a tiny dent on the Old Firm, finishing above Rangers once, before they were liquidated due to their own horrendous non-payment of bills. Hearts never got close to Celtic, and made only one other cup final, the 2013 League Cup which they surprisingly lost 3-2 to St Mirren. Where they did leave more than a dent, however, was on their great rivals' ego and psyche, and so in that respect it is easy to see why Romanov's many, many faults are glossed over by the Hearts support. They might have expected more for the money they spent, but when one of them was that 5-1 cup final it's hard to complain. Especially as it wasn't their money they spent anyway.

* * *

There is a postscript to the way the Romanov era ended and its effect on the Edinburgh rivalry. In a brilliant illustration of how rivalries can work, a rumour grew among the Hearts support that Hibernian fans were trying to scupper the deals and meetings happening in Lithuania that would save Hearts. The insolvency case was proceeding, and Hearts were desperately trying to reach a deal to save the club, and Tynecastle. One Hearts fan, Steve Weddell, wrote in his memoir of the time, 'Not insignificant numbers of Hibs fans pestering the authorities in Lithuania, inundating them with reasons to reject the Foundation of Hearts' bid to secure the Ubig (Hearts' Lithuanian holding company) shares … it became a concerted effort to see their oldest, bitterest rivals liquidated out of all existence.'

It is very believable that there would be Hibernian fans trying to make mischief in the process; after all, Hearts had tried to liquidate Hibernian out of all existence in 1990. But, equally, the accounts of Hearts supporters from that time do seem to fixate on, and inflate, the significance of it. Given the complexities of unwinding the nefarious financial shenanigans that Hearts had been involved in for almost a decade – tens of millions of pounds of loans from shell companies, multiple debt for equality swaps and everything else that make financial collapses so complicated to unravel – dealing with spam emails – even if there were 'a lot' – doesn't seem like it would figure high on the big list of issues to be dealt with to stop this deal collapsing.

The suggestions that this was happening first surfaced in the media based on sources in Lithuania citing 'private individuals' sending emails to try and influence the way that creditors would vote, and it quickly became one of the dominant narratives among Hearts supporters. It was the Scottish media who said they were Hibernian supporters, not anyone in Lithuania. The accusations were reiterated by politician and former chair of the Foundation of Hearts, Ian Murray MP, who made the point in his book about the rescue that he was told by one of the Lithuanian administrators they were having to respond to 'a lot' of spam emails questioning the validity of the deal.

It's hard not to wonder how much it was simply to drag Hibernian into the mess, in order to give the supporters a scapegoat, a hate figure against which to vent their fury, a focal point for their frustration. Far easier to rally against an evil plot by Hibernian supporters than it would be against some faceless administrators or nameless suits in Lithuania. Or worse, against the Hearts men who had willingly taken Romanov's money in exchange for their shares in the club, lauding him and encouraging others to do likewise. That they were now firmly behind the movement trying to clean up the mess they had been complicit in inflicting upon their club meant they couldn't be blamed. And the Hearts support were still reluctant to really criticise Romanov himself, perhaps out of fear of his vindictiveness, perhaps out of some residual affection for the journey he had taken them on. But the notion that this was the Hearts fans fighting against Hibernian and a 'concerted effort' by 'not insignificant numbers' of people who were probably Hibernian fans worked brilliantly, and it has now been woven into the very fabric of the story.

While I don't doubt that the vast majority of Hibernian supporters would have loved to have seen their rivals collapse to one degree or another – as one said to me when talking about this period, 'I hoped they would die as a club and never be spoken about again' – but wishing it to be so and being able to make it so are very different things. As with the myths around Celtic and Hibernian way back in the late 19th century, it's often easier to blame someone else than be confronted by the failings of your own club and your fellow supporters; all fans do it. And while it added to the sense of fever pitch around the derby, I think Hibernian supporters' place in the rogues' gallery responsible for bringing Hearts to their knees is a very minor one.

The Romanov era was characterised by a lot of self-important people who self-aggrandised and back-slapped themselves, even as they were doing about-turns on their previous positions. There were lots of people who made lots of money out of Romanov, and even more who facilitated his reign, and its calamitous end. So I wanted to end the Romanov reign by focusing on the people that really matter, the supporters, because that's where the Romanov story ultimately ended up, with them owning their club.

A couple of days after speaking to Neil, I was sitting thinking about our conversation, going over it all again in my head, thinking about dodgy share offers, whether or not he really believed they could challenge in Europe, Mad Vlad and all the rest of the circus. I realised I hadn't asked him the most simple question, so I texted him to ask.

'All things considered, was it worth it?'

'Yes,' he replied.

CHAPTER 18

PAYING THE PRICE

2012–2019

THE HIGH of Hearts' Scottish Cup demolition of Hibernian is unlikely to be bettered, and although it will always be with the fans, it didn't last long for the club as the reality of their situation started to become more dire, on and off the pitch. Hibernian actually recovered from this heavy blow fairly well. Fate drew them together in the third round the very next season, meaning Hearts' first match in defence of their trophy came at Easter Road, Hibs winning a forgettable game 1-0 and making it all the way to the final before losing again, this time 3-0 to Celtic; an unlikely cup run for the second season running, but with a very predictable ending.

Hearts fans were still basking in the glow of victory, but off the pitch they had other things to worry about, as their dire financial situation became more apparent and the Romanov house of cards started to collapse. Hearts finished season 2012/13 poorly, and had they gone into administration then (which many suspected they were on the brink of doing) they might have been relegated with

242

the resulting 15-point penalty. They limped through to the summer, however, when the inevitable happened and they accepted that they were not going to be able to pay back their debts, entering administration in 2013 just after the season was completed. Hearts finished third bottom, while Hibernian finished seventh, with 13 wins, 13 defeats and 12 draws. As a result of getting to the Scottish Cup Final, Hibs qualified for the Europa League preliminaries, which seemed like a bonus outcome from a poor season; it didn't turn out that way though.

Hibernian played Malmo and, after losing the first leg in Sweden 2-0, delivered one of their most humiliating performances ever, losing at home 7-0. It was a tough one to take, and their manager Pat Fenlon never really recovered from the result. Of course, it was Hearts who would deliver the final blow. Drawn together in the League Cup quarter-finals at Easter Road, Hibernian came storming out the traps and looked like they were going to blow their rivals away, hitting the post and the bar in the opening minutes. Then out of nowhere, Hearts scored, and then succeeded in deflating the ground and their opponents, and holding on for the most unlikely of victories. In many ways, it was the archetypal Hearts derby result, and illustrated a major reason for Hearts' strong derby record. As one Hibernian fan put to me, 'I think Hearts' better record in the derbies – certainly in the last 40 years that I've been watching – is that they win the matches they should win, when they are clearly better. But they are also good at getting results when they should lose, when they are struggling or Hibs are flying. Hard-fought draws usually, but also the odd against-the-run-of-play win.' It's a point also made by Tony, the neutral Edinburgh football fan, who remarked, 'It seemed the script was Hibs would play all the football but Hearts would win with a deflected shot in the 80th minute. That's how I remember it anyway.' It wasn't the only example of Hearts' resilience in derby matches that season.

Hearts never threatened to overturn their 15-point penalty, and were destined for relegation from early in the season. What was more of a surprise was that Hibernian would conspire to join them there. With a disastrous managerial appointment, Hibernian went from mid-table mediocrity to relegation candidates, plummeting to second bottom with a 13-match winless run, including six defeats in a row. This run included a match at Tynecastle, where, as fate would have it, Hibernian had the chance to relegate Hearts with a victory.

It was a classic derby match; Hearts gained nothing from winning, other than to hurt their rivals, and drag them down with them (although Hibernian that season were such a shambles, they didn't take much dragging). It was delightfully petty and parochial, laden with spite; everything you want from a derby match. It also meant that for the first time in its 139-year history, the Edinburgh Derby would take place in the second tier (the Championship) of the Scottish league.

The inevitability around Hearts' relegation meant that they were well prepared for what was to be the hardest second tier in history, because Hearts and Hibernian were meeting Rangers, on their way back up after going bust and starting again at the bottom of the leagues and only one of them could be promoted automatically, with one other into a play-off. Hearts got off to a great start, beating Rangers at Ibrox, and never looked back, romping to the title in surprisingly easy fashion, including a 10-0 win at home against Cowdenbeath. Hibernian slowly recovered under new manager Alan Stubbs, and finished above Rangers in second place, only to lose to them in the play-offs. The derbies that season were a barometer of where the two teams were, with Hearts winning the first 2-1 before two 1-1 draws, with Hibs winning the last 2-0 at Easter Road, but Hibernian and Rangers would remain in the second tier for season 2015/16 to fight it out for promotion again.

Hearts did more than just consolidate upon their return to the top flight, and as a sign of the progress they were making off the pitch under owner Ann Budge, they finished in an impressive third place and qualified for Europe. And just as it seemed as if there would be a season without Edinburgh Derbies, the Scottish Cup fifth round sent Hibernian to Tynecastle. Hibs were fighting it out with Rangers and Falkirk for promotion, but in what turned out to be an amazing season, they made it to both major cup finals. But the toil of that season seemed to be scuppering their chances in the cruellest way possible – Hibernian lost the League Cup Final to Ross County, conceding a last-minute winner, and in the promotion play-offs they lost to Falkirk, also conceding a last-minute winner the midweek before they were due at Hampden to play Rangers in the Scottish Cup Final, the first ever to feature two teams from outside the top division.

Hearts raced into a two-goal lead, and all seemed well with the world from a Hearts perspective. They had dragged them down with them, overtaken them on the way back up, and were now about to rub salt into Hibernian's Scottish Cup wound. But the greens slowly fought their way back and took control of the match, pulling a goal back in the 80th minute, and equalising in injury time to take the match to a replay at Easter Road, a match they would win 1-0. Despite being the league below, and two goals down, Hibernian had come back to knock Hearts out of the Scottish Cup; and it was to be Hibs who got to rub salt into the wound.

In the 2016 Scottish Cup Final, Hibernian, driven on by the mercurial Anthony Stokes, put in a sparkling display and were a goal up after just a couple of minutes through Stokes. Rangers, who were looking for their first major trophy since their own staggering demise, fought back and just after half-time scored to go 2-1 up, and so it stayed until the 80th minute, when Stokes equalised. They would go one better than their late comeback at Tynecastle though, and in the 92nd minute they scored the winner to take the Scottish Cup for the first time in 114 years. The significance of that cup win to Hibernian is difficult to overstate – there have been four different books published about it – and that they beat Hearts en route brought in a bit of local rivalry to this story. For Hibernian it was redemption in the most dramatic manner possible. For Hearts, they had to watch their rivals end their curse and lament their own part in making it possible.

The 2016/17 season saw Hibernian ride the crest of their wave and win promotion at the third time of asking. Hearts had an indifferent season, finishing fifth and outside the European places. They also drew Hibernian at home again in the Scottish Cup fifth round. This time the two clubs fought out a 0-0 draw, with Hibernian content to bring the replay back to Easter Road. Again, lower-league Hibernian defeated their rivals although it was more convincing this time, 3-1, and Hibs got back to Hampden to defend their trophy, eventually losing 3-2 to Aberdeen in the semi-final.

With their promotion, the Edinburgh Derby would be back as a top-flight fixture in season 2017/18, and amazingly the two clubs were drawn to play each other at Tynecastle in the Scottish Cup for the third season running, Hearts winning this one 1-0 for their first win in ten derby matches. They otherwise finished sixth, in what was another mediocre season, with Hibernian finishing fourth after a thrilling last match when they drew with Rangers 5-5 at Easter Road. Hibernian won both derby matches at Easter Road, while Hearts got one league victory and one Scottish Cup victory at Tynecastle, and drew the other home match.

Hearts had descended into a spiral of mediocrity under their new ownership, and would finish sixth again in season 2018/19. It was perhaps an inevitable consequence, a comedown after the adrenaline-fuelled years of administration and recovery, and the Romanov years before that, which were lots of things, but never dull. Hearts were in a post-excitement lull, but they didn't seem to know how to get out of it – quite the opposite, in fact. At Easter Road, their rivals were starting to do likewise and, since their first season back in the top flight in 2017/18, had finished fourth and fifth. Hearts did make it to the Scottish Cup Final this season, but despite taking the lead early in the second half, they lost 2-1 to Celtic. It was a chance for Hearts to properly put the last few years behind them and reward their loyal support with a trophy, but in truth, and as is so often the case now, it was a mismatch, and a mediocre Hearts side did well to give Celtic a close game. The cup was not to be, although there would be another chance not far away, just the other side of one of the most bitter and controversial episodes in the modern history of Scottish football; an episode that Hearts were to find themselves right at the centre of.

CHAPTER 19

WHAT TIMES WE LIVE IN

2019–2023

THE 2019/20 season started brightly, and both Hibernian and Hearts made it to the League Cup semi-finals, setting up the enticing prospect of a first all-Edinburgh League Cup Final, but both clubs were laid low by the Old Firm, Hibernian losing 5-2 to Celtic while Hearts lost 3-0 to Rangers. The season will mostly be remembered for being incomplete due to the Covid pandemic, and it was abandoned in March 2020 as the severity of Covid became apparent. As we all faced weeks of being locked inside our homes, the authorities had to find a way to decide on how to end the season, and they chose average points per game, meaning that Hearts were relegated for the second time in six years. With 30 (out of 38) games played, they were bottom, four points adrift from second bottom with just four league wins all season, and having just lost to two of their relegation rivals, St Mirren and Hamilton Academical. Hearts were furious at the outcome, and fought incredibly hard off the pitch to have the decision overturned, despite looking likely to be relegated anyway.

The difficulty facing the league was that they wanted to award the prizes (and the money that went with them) to help clubs through the pandemic; Celtic were desperate to equal the nine-titles-in-a-row record, and Dundee United had just won the Championship and were desperate to be promoted. But for promotion to happen, there had to be relegation, and that's where Hearts came in. This was a huge blow to them, not just in that it would put a potential hole in their finances just as they were recovering from their previous relegation and administration. It meant a second relegation in six years, their fifth since the advent of the Scottish Premier Division in 1975, having gone their entire history without ever being relegated up until season 1977. This was a huge blow to their prestige, and one suspects this was as much as anything behind their extraordinary efforts to overturn the decision.

Their anger was aimed at the way in which a vital vote on using points per game as the basis on which to decide final league positions was handled, which was objectively bad. Dundee's vote was late, and was then changed. Hearts were furious.

From their point of view, they were being unfairly penalised, and they rightly pointed out that nobody could know how the remaining eight matches would have gone, On the other side, when neither finishing the season nor postponing it indefinitely was an option, using the fairest and most accurate indicator of each team's merit, i.e. the league table, seemed liked the least bad solution. But, of course, the clubs that were losing out – Hearts, Partick

Thistle and Stranraer – were angry at being relegated using points per game. Hibernian voted for the proposal – despite it meaning they were moved down a place in the league – but their fans would have gone ballistic at their club had they, in any way, been seen to be helping Hearts out of a hole. An independent tribunal ratified the decision, but that didn't calm things down, so in response the league gave Hearts owner Ann Budge the opportunity to work up proposals for reconstruction of the leagues that would minimise the harm inflicted upon clubs, which would be voted on by all member clubs. Her campaign to reconstruct Scottish football was for the good of the Scottish game she said, but to absolutely nobody's surprise the main takeaway from the plans was a solution that didn't involve Hearts being relegated. This was supported by only 16 of the 42 league clubs, who were never likely to back a wholesale reorganisation of the leagues in Scottish football just to prevent Hearts getting relegated.

Football clubs are of course not always the most rational institutions, and in what became a brilliant example of club group-think and online echo-chambers at work, Hearts and their media supporters whipped themselves into a frenzy of indignance, convincing themselves that the decision would be overturned, or that the obvious justice of their point of view would be recognised in the courts and they would be awarded millions in compensation for having been wronged. How much of this was genuine on the part of the club, and how much was performative for the benefit of their supporters, we will never know. But when the reconstruction proposal fell, Hearts announced they would be taking legal action, with thinly disguised vitriol aimed at their fellow clubs:

> To say we are disappointed, yet sadly not surprised, at this outcome is, of course, an understatement. We have, from the outset, worked tirelessly with fellow clubs and the SPFL Board to try to find a solution that would right the most obvious wrongs ... Hearts, along with many others, have stated repeatedly that no club should be disproportionately disadvantaged because of this crisis. This was the final opportunity for kinship to prevail and for Scottish football to stand together in an emergency. It is an unfortunate condemnation of Scottish football that this was not possible.
>
> We thank those who were open-minded, pragmatic and willing to come together to try and reach a fair outcome for all. Sadly, there were too few of us ... we are left with no choice but to proceed with a legal challenge. The club has tried throughout these last few months to avoid this course of action but we must now do the right thing by our supporters, our employees, our players and our sponsors, all of whom have been unwavering in their commitment and support.
>
> We can hold our heads up high as we have acted at all times with integrity, common sense

and with the best interests of Scottish football at heart. We have stated from the beginning that the unjust and unfair treatment of Hearts, Partick Thistle, Stranraer and indeed other clubs cannot be allowed to go unchallenged. While many weeks have been wasted in trying to find a solution, we must now formally challenge this outcome.

Despite Hearts being very confident in their legal case, the Court of Session in Edinburgh delivered a 'clear, comprehensive and unanimous' verdict against Hearts and Partick Thistle, and vindicated the decisions and actions of the league. Hearts and Partick Thistle's demands for £10m in compensation were also dismissed by the court. Their relegation, which had now dragged on for months, was confirmed for the second time, and Hearts once again found themselves in the second tier of Scottish football for the start of season 2020/21. It was an unedifying case for Hearts, and leaving complicated legal arguments to one side, to most fans it was a simple case of the worst team in the league trying whatever they could to escape relegation. There was, however, one last matter hanging over from the Covid-disrupted season that required tidying up, the small matter of a Scottish Cup semi-final between Hearts and Hibernian.

This was held over to the start of the next season, and a tight game was 1-1 going into the last few minutes when Hibernian were awarded a penalty. Kevin Nisbet crashed it off the bar. When Hearts were subsequently awarded a penalty in extra time, Liam Boyce didn't miss and Hearts went through to the final, where, in an amazing match, they lost on penalties to Celtic. Hearts came from two goals down, then 3-2 down in extra time, to find themselves two kicks to the good in the penalty shoot-out. Amazingly, they conspired to miss their remaining penalties, allowing Celtic to take the trophy. It was a sore one to lose for Hearts, who had the trophy in their grasp and, as with the previous season's final, lost from a winning position against Celtic. They did of course gain some revenge over Hibernian, knocking them out as a lower league club and maintaining their formidable derby record at Hampden. They went on to win the Championship and promotion fairly easily, and ensure they came back up. Hibernian for their part took to the strange Covid season of no supporters in stadiums well – cynics suggested they did well because of a lack of supporters in grounds, particularly at home! – and finished third for the first time since 2005 and reached the Scottish Cup Final, where a particularly underwhelming performance saw them lose 1-0 to St Johnstone, who remarkably did the cup double (they also beat Hibernian 3-0 in the League Cup semi-final).

Typically, Hibernian didn't follow up their strong season, and their league form faltered at the start of season 2021/22, their season seemingly derailed early after a UEFA Europa League qualifier defeat to Croatian side HNK Rijeka. They did produce one of the great modern-day cup performances, and kept up their bizarrely strong record against Rangers at Hampden, by beating them 3-1 in the League Cup semi-final to earn the right to face Celtic in the final. Hibernian sacked their manager, Jack Ross, due to indifferent league form and supporter unrest with his style of play, the week before the League Cup Final. Despite this self-inflicted damage, Hibernian actually took the lead, but conspired to concede an equaliser straight from the restart in what was a shocking lack of concentration, before losing the match 2-1. Going one goal up in that final turned out to be a highlight, as the season drifted along to a disappointing eighth-placed finish.

Hearts on the other hand had come back up from the Championship with renewed vigour – and I suspect a sense of grievance burning away within. They took the top flight by storm, finishing third. But the highlight of the season came in yet another Scottish Cup date with Hibernian. For two rivals who had barely met in Scottish Cups for decades, they were making up for lost time.

Hearts defeated their rivals 2-1 at Hampden, thanks to one very good goal, and one absolutely world-class goal from a free kick. Hibernian hit back, and actually had the better of the second half, but as had so often been their undoing that season, they had little cutting edge. Hearts were through to their third final in six seasons, and they were building quite the record in Hampden matches against their great rivals; in fact, Hibernian have never beaten Hearts at Hampden, albeit they have only played four times there.

Hearts would once again face the Old Firm in the final, and this time it was Rangers who defeated them 2-0 after extra time. This one was easier to take, as unlike those two recent finals versus Celtic, Hearts never looked like they were going to win this one. Hearts had the huge consolation of their third-place finish giving them automatic entry to the UEFA Europa Conference League.

In truth, their European run dominated the early part of their season in 2022/23, and despite taking a few hidings (including from eventual runners-up Fiorentina), Hearts put in what could reasonably be considered a par performance, finishing third in their group behind Fiorentina and Istanbul Basaksehir. Importantly, it gave them an enormous financial boost over their two main rivals for third, Aberdeen and Hibernian. Despite being 12 points in front at one stage, Hearts went on a spectacular collapse towards the end of the season, allowing Aberdeen to finish third – and win the riches of the Conference League. They only just managed to hold on to fourth, after Hibernian made a late charge, but a battling 1-1 draw – Hearts playing most of the match with ten men – allowed them to cling on, meaning both clubs qualified for the preliminary rounds, meaning both clubs were fairly happy. In theory at least …

At full time, Hibernian manager Lee Johnson gave a perfunctory handshake to Hearts manager Steven Naismith, but then makes a half grab (or else he said something that wasn't audible to cameras). Naismith reacted, and the two squared up, igniting a 'mass brawl' that saw four people sent off – Johnson himself, two unused substitutes (one from each side) and Hearts' goalkeeping coach – and involved virtually every player and member of the coaching staff. As always with football 'brawls' it looked worse than it was, but it did show that these matches still get the blood pumping in players and staff, as well as fans.

Interestingly, and in a nod to history that I'm sure was entirely unintentional, Lee Johnson afterwards talked about the dislike between him and Hearts manager Stephen Naismith, and how there was a bit of 'needle' between them. I'm sure Messrs Purdie, Whelahan and those 'Hibernian roughs' who destroyed that cab back in 1878 would have approved.

CHAPTER 20

EPILOGUE: THE NATURAL ORDER?

IT'S MARCH 2018, and Hibernian striker Jamie Maclaren has just scored Hibernian's second goal of the evening, a scrappy, proper striker's goal from close range. Hibernian's first that evening was the opposite, a beautiful left-foot daisy-cutter of a half-volley from the edge of the box. Two-nil up, and the Hearts fans had started to leave the stadium. With the match nearing its end, the Hibernian fans on the top tier of the Famous Five stand behind the goals unfurled a large green banner which hung down, and in huge white letters it read simply, 'Natural Order?' It was of course a response to Craig Levein's comments following the previous derby match, which Hearts won 1-0. This victory for Hibernian moved them 12 points clear of their city rivals, and although they didn't know it at the time, it was the first year in a run of four consecutive seasons that they would finish above Hearts in the league.

The thing about that line that worked so well, that caught the imagination so much, was that it works on so many levels. It alludes to Hearts' dominance in the 80s and

90s; it alludes to Hearts being the Edinburgh establishment team, and Hibernian as the outsiders. It has hints of the Romanov-era 'big team, wee team' patter. For Hibernian fans, it speaks to the unacknowledged forces in the city that they have always felt worked against them; their place as outsiders; but also with the inclusion of that single question mark, it brings them back to smashing that established order in the 60s and 70s and turned it on its head. It is a line that both sets of supporters can identity with, and will no doubt return to again and again. For this book, it raises an obvious question: what is the Natural Order in Edinburgh? It's a difficult question to answer, because 150 years of history creates a lot of nuance, a lot of shades of grey.

Much of the current rivalry has been shaped, possibly defined, by the Romanov era and the years immediately before and after. Romanov was a nefarious character, but by luck or judgement, his period and his style chimed with the Hearts support, a support whose very foundations as the bastion of Edinburgh were being shaken by constant off-field struggles and financial difficulty. Basically, their financial means were struggling to match their own expectations. Romanov changed that, by giving them free rein to spend their way back to what Hearts see as their rightful place, and what's more, it was done almost directly at the expense of Hibernian.

When Hearts finished above them in 2005, it confirmed their superiority (Hibernian had finished third in 2004). When the two clubs were drawn to play at Hampden in the Scottish Cup semi-final in 2006, it was a direct clash of the two approaches. A Hibernian team full of young players and English lower-league journeymen (basically all the club could afford at that time) against a Hearts at the peak of their powers. The trend was set, and despite the Romanov revolution quickly losing its financial power, Hearts managed to confirm it in 2012 in *that* cup final, which was epoch-defining for Hearts, and in their minds absolutely cemented their place as Edinburgh's club. Hibs only compounded the sense of a zero-sum game by conspiring to achieve the most unlikely of relegations in 2014 when Hearts were relegated, in effect sharing Hearts' punishment for the years of financial doping.

And yet Hibernian swallowed that calamitous relegation, and like the motto of Leith, they persevered. Not only did they persevere, they came within one match of a cup double – as a second-tier team, an incredible feat. And in winning the Scottish Cup against Rangers in 2016, Hibernian exorcised their own demons, ending their incredible barren run. The fact that Hibernian's calamitous history in the tournament had become such a pillar of Hearts supporters' sense of superiority over their rivals only added to the incredible release that Scottish football witnessed. That pitch invasion was a huge cathartic outpouring, which told the rest of Scottish football who had been laughing at them (often with lots of justification) that despite being down, they were most definitely not out. The fact Hibernian had knocked out Hearts en route in a dramatic (and for Hearts, calamitous) manner only heightened that sense of karma, of revenge.

There was a further blow to Hearts' prestige, when they were relegated under a controversial average points per game calculation when the league was cut short by Covid. Hearts reacted with fury, and in what became a long, drawn-out saga, fought tooth and nail, including suing the other clubs involved to seek damages. It was unedifying and ultimately fruitless. For a club with pretensions to be the third most successful in Scotland, this was a blow to that self-image. Their biggest rivals for the third most successful club title, Aberdeen, have never been relegated (although they were saved once by a technicality). As football journalist Alan Pattullo pointed out in *The Scotsman*, since the advent of the Premier League in 1975, Hearts are now the joint most-relegated club, dropping down an astonishing five times since 1977, twice more than Hibernian, and five times more than Aberdeen.

Ultimately, Hearts' singular identity as Edina's Darlings is more threatened by Hibernian than Hibernian's identity is by Hearts. In the modern 21st century, Hearts have no built-in demographic advantage over Hibernian anymore. They aren't seen as Edinburgh's champions against a feared, disliked or misunderstood religious minority anymore. They can't rest on their laurels and just be 'Edinburgh's club' anymore. Hibernian have – against the odds at times – established themselves to be as much a part of Edinburgh as Hearts are. In theory, Hibernian could usurp Hearts' identity; they could, in theory at least, dominate derbies and win more trophies and become the dominant force in the city. That's not to say that will happen, but the point is it's a possibility, it's a threat that before World War Two didn't exist. The weird paradox is that this threat doesn't cut both ways.

Because Hearts can't threaten Hibernian's identity in the same way – Hibernian's identity, a balance between their Catholic Irish, Leith and Edinburgh heritage, has been contested and problematic, but that has come from within. Hearts couldn't – nor indeed would they want to – challenge two of those identities. They have tried to challenge the Edinburgh part and perhaps this is why Hearts have twice tried to defeat Hibernian off the pitch, trying – and failing by just one vote – to have them expelled from the Edinburgh FA in the 1880s; and then trying, and narrowly failing again, to buy them over and close them down in 1990. Hearts always seem to have approached Hibernian with more animosity at an official level; so many instances in this 150 years' history bring back those fateful words that were spoken to Hearts, trying to cheat the rules on professionalism to get an edge on their opponents before a Scottish Cup tie: 'Let it cost what it will.'

Hibernian are the historic underdogs of the rivalry, traditionally a poorer and, for much of the first half of their existence, the smaller of the clubs, drawing their support from a much narrower pool of potential supporters and being associated with a religion that was alien to the vast majority of Edinburghers. The post-war years have seen this position change and improve. Edinburgh has continued to grow as a city, Hibernian's traditional areas of support were the subjects of slum clearances that spread it over a much wider geographical base in the city. And as Edinburgh has secularised, in a way that wouldn't have seemed possible early in the 20th century, their identity, with which they struggled for so many years, is far more settled, and far less contentious. The reasons that people become Hibernian supporters are different and reflect the different identities of the club. In Andy MacVannan's book *We are Hibernian*, he interviews Hibernian fans (both famous and not famous) about their thoughts on the club, and how they became Hibbies. Seven cited family/their father, four cited Leith specifically, three cited Irish/Catholic identity, two cited Leith Catholic identity, one more cited a Leith/Southside identity and five had various random reasons. A totally unscientific sample size, but it shows a fairly even split between the Irish Catholic identity and the Leith identity.

In that sense, Hibernian Football Club have shared the fate of their traditional community; they have successfully integrated, they have become part of their city; their Irish Catholic heritage is not instead of their Edinburgh identity anymore – they have become one and the same. Cities evolve, and Edinburgh evolved to include a Catholic Irish minority within its people, just as it has done with Leith and Leithers.

For Hearts, being the establishment club is both a strength and a potential weakness. The trouble with being Edina's Darlings is that they cannot increase that, it can only be maintained – which by its nature makes their identity slightly defensive. At the start of World War Two they were clearly Scotland's third force; by the

1960s, they were being challenged by Hibernian in their home city. And just as Celtic changed the dynamic of Edinburgh football from afar by hobbling Hibernian, so Hearts (and Hibernian) have faced the challenge of Aberdeen. The Dons weren't a major challenger until the war, but since defeating Hibernian in the 1946/47 Scottish Cup Final, Aberdeen have not only caught up with Hearts and Hibernian, they have overtaken both clubs in the number of major trophies won.[58] In terms of all-time top-flight league points won, Hearts remain third, Aberdeen are fourth and Hibernian are fifth. This is despite Aberdeen not being created until 1903 (making them 28/29 years younger than the Edinburgh rivals). Their accelerating challenge to the Edinburgh clubs really becomes apparent when looking at the top division points won up until 1975 (the old Division One); Hearts are clear in third, Hibernian are fourth and Aberdeen sit behind Dundee, Motherwell and Partick Thistle in eighth. The same league table since 1975 (the advent of the Premier Division) shows Aberdeen clear third, Hearts have dropped back to fourth, and Dundee United and Motherwell sit above Hibernian in seventh.

Since the 1960s Hearts have been a club in decline relative to their rivals, who have challenged their place in Scottish football in a way that didn't happen pre-war – and in Aberdeen's case have taken their place as the most successful club – the third force, since World War Two. The gap between the Edinburgh rivals in the league has also narrowed significantly since World War Two. Hearts finished above their Edinburgh rivals 31 times (Hibernian finished higher only 15 times) in the 46 seasons between Hibernian being admitted to the league in 1894 and the outbreak of war in 1939. In the 77 seasons played since,[59] Hearts have finished above their great rivals 41 times, but Hibernian have turned the tables 36 times. In the same period Hearts have won ten of Scotland's major trophies (four Scottish Cups, four League Cups, two league flags) and Hibernian have won seven (one Scottish Cup, three League Cups, three league flags), and for the first time since Celtic were created in 1888, Hearts and their supporters have had to live through periods of Hibernian dominance. To a club whose whole identity has been built upon being the top dog in Edinburgh, and the third-biggest/most-successful club in the country, what does seeing that position eroded do to their sense of who they are? None of this is to say Hearts have fallen away, and they are arguably Scotland's 'third force' – but the point is it's arguable now in a way it wasn't previously.

From the perspective of the Edinburgh Derby, this has probably helped to increase the intensity, as the bragging rights that come with winning derbies or dominating the rival increase in importance. In many ways the derby matches have become the Castle Rock of Hearts' identity, immovable and impregnable, even as Hibernian drew level and Aberdeen overtook them in other spheres. As their formidable record in derbies continues, so too can their claim to be the top dog in the city, and their place as Edina's Darlings remains. While the last few years have seen the derby matches see-saw in a much more normal way, winning a few then losing a few, such is Hearts' historic lead that Hibernian would need years of dominance to close it; not something that looks likely to happen. According to the London Hearts supporters' club website, as it stands up to the end of season 2022/23, there have been 660 Edinburgh Derbies played; Hearts have won 290 of them, Hibernian have won 207, 157 have been draws and six matches have been abandoned. This includes all of the local competitions, minor competitions and 'friendlies'. In what are recognised as the three main competitions – league, League Cup and Scottish Cup – the total matches played is 355; Hearts have won 154 and Hibernian have won 99, and 102 have been draws.

But if Hearts are being challenged, their fans have shown they are up for it. With the help of Edinburgh businesswoman Ann Budge, they rescued Hearts from the carcass of the Romanov empire, and have resuscitated it, and while Budge and other benefactors have helped considerably by donating money, it is the fans who effectively paid for it, and who now own it. Since their Foundation of Hearts takeover in 2021, they have spent around £15m on their club, and continue to do so – a truly remarkable effort. As for Romanov, he was charged with a raft of criminal offences (which he denied) and is now living in Russia, fighting extradition attempts by Lithuania.

So what does the future hold for the Edinburgh Derby?

Lots of the materials I read and people I spoke to talked about Hibernian and Hearts needing each other.

I'm not sure I understand what that means, even now. They are certainly important to one another, and much of their history has been influenced by each other. Mackie's history of Hearts devotes a whole chapter to the 'Edinburgh Rivals', and Hibs are mentioned on the first page of the first chapter of the book. Hearts are mentioned on page two of the first chapter of Mackay's history of Hibernian and on page seven of Hibernian's centenary history *100 Years of Hibs*. Football fans take a greater interest in their rivals than almost any other team apart from their own. It never fails to amaze me how many Hearts and Hibernian supporters will leave contributions online, boldly stating how one or other are *'obsessed with us'*, or how such and such is *'living rent free'* inside their heads, completely oblivious to the irony of making fun of your rival fans' obsession over you, by talking and thinking about your rivals! Rivals are generally obsessed with one another; trying to brag about not being bothered by them on a story or a thread that is *specifically discussing them* only reinforces that point. But what does 'need each other' mean?

If either Hibernian or Hearts didn't exist, would the other wither away to become some minor club, devoid of intra-city competition? Almost certainly not. The nature of their history and their self-identity might change, but why would they struggle any more than, say, Newcastle United or, dare I say, Aberdeen? Or even clubs with an asymmetrical derby, like Aston Villa or Nottingham Forest? Edinburgh football would definitely be a less interesting place without the rivalry, but I see no evidence that either club relies on the other to exist – far from it, they are direct competitors.

One of the unintended – but actually very welcome – consequences of Scottish football's relative impoverishment is that while it has missed out on many of the good things about modern football, it's also managed to avoid some of the pitfalls. And it is one of the contradictions of football in Edinburgh – that a city that is so outwardly and obviously successful in being prosperous, educated, cosmopolitan, interesting and cultural retains a football rivalry that is relatively untouched by these aspects of its home city. To witness the Edinburgh rivals – not least when they play each other – is to see a different Edinburgh. Not necessarily a more real Edinburgh, but a very different Edinburgh. Hibernian were more famous for their large and notorious hooligan gang – the Capital City Service or CCS – than they are for links to their home city's successful industries. And yet the two would clash when, in 1990, they played a part in dissuading Wallace Mercer, backed by cash borrowed from the Bank of Scotland – headquartered in Edinburgh for hundreds of years – from continuing with Hearts' takeover attempt. The Jekyll and Hyde city, where 80s yuppies flush with borrowed cash run up against casuals in designer clothes and a van full of petrol bombs.

Both clubs have managed to remain in their historic homes, and both are still called their historic names and not named after big global companies; in fact they are not named after any companies at all. When the chairwoman and financial saviour of Hearts, Ann Budge, first announced that the club would remain at Tynecastle and complete its redevelopment, she was asked about the possibility of selling the naming rights to the ground. She told the BBC, 'I don't think we'd like it to be called anything other than Tynecastle.'[60] Nor are the grounds awash with large corporate sponsors. The advertising boards around the pitches are as likely to feature the name of a local plumbing firm or restaurant as they are a multi-national. And you will not find any adverts in Vietnamese, Thai or Mandarin.

And while there are of course plenty of well-to-do and successful individuals who attend matches, the crowds en masse represent the Edinburgh of council-housing estates and the old inner-city slums; the traditional working-class areas of the city, in which the clubs remain rooted. While world-famous writer Irvine Welsh is a well-known Hibernian fan, the warts-and-all Edinburgh of his novels can be just as relatable to fans of Hearts and can be just as evocative of districts of Edinburgh that are traditionally more associated with them. And in both grounds you will find groups of youngsters (and some not so young) organised into bunches of 'ultras' who sing and bring colour and noise to the matches (a recent import from Europe that has really shaken up Scottish fan culture).

There is potential here though. For the opening home league games of the season 2023/24, Hibernian had a crowd of circa 17,500 versus St Mirren, and Hearts had a crowd of around 19,000 versus Kilmarnock. Both of these are on the high side by historical standards; in the 90s, home crowds of around 9,000 or 10,000 would be fairly standard. Hearts have reduced their allocation for away supporters and sold out their season tickets for the year. And to reiterate, this is for a competition that 100 per cent of those fans know they cannot win, that third is the best they can hope for. Such crowds would put them firmly in the medium-sized European club category. The resilience and commitment of the non-Old Firm Scottish football fan is incredible. But despite the relative health of both clubs both on and off the field, you don't have to dig far to find negative notes.

As much as the fans will go to support their clubs, the unrelenting nothingness of Scottish football does seem to take its toll. While it is obviously a reflection of how structurally rigged the Scottish game is, and how thoroughly mind-numbingly, soul-crushingly boring that is for fans, it is possibly a reflection of more recent changes in English and European football. As money warps the game more and more, what is the future of domestic football? We already have three European leagues (of sorts), a Super League of some description seems inevitable, and in Scotland, we are in the strange and unenviable position of sharing a country (technically) with the largest, best-marketed and richest football league in the world; of course that has an effect on Scottish fans – how could it not? There was reflexive uproar when the Super League plans came to light, just as there is when the Old Firm periodically float their next big idea to leave Scotland. But there must come a point when we all have to accept that some clubs have become too big for their domestic game, and that supranational competition is required. But where would that leave the Edinburgh Derby? What we can be sure of is Hibernian won't be pioneering this European competition, and instead, both they and Hearts will be tossed about in the wake of the European super-clubs, like all of the other mid-sized clubs in medium and small countries around the continent.

It's hard not to think that Hibernian found something of a happy home in Europe, and that the rise of European club competitions came at just the right time for them. A club searching for an identity found it in those nights, where the attacking style of play developed in the 40s and 50s found expression – and utility – in a succession of unlikely home results. The rousing, one-off occasion in front of huge crowds at Easter Road suited their mercurial style, and often the performances of those sides went above and beyond what they displayed in run-of-the-mill Scottish football. Hearts' more certain identity as 'Edinburgh's club' meant they needed no affirmation from European adventures, and as much as they celebrated their victories when they did come along, it was just never as central to them. The fact that European football really took off at a time when Hearts were entering a long slump obviously didn't help either. If football is to become more European in its set-up in the future, what that will do to both clubs' sense of identity and how they are will be fascinating to watch – but maybe that's one for someone writing on the Edinburgh's Derby's 250th anniversary.

One of the main questions I have been asked by people while writing is the inevitable question: who is bigger, what is the *natural order*? I think I would answer now that there have been three distinct phases. At the outset, Hibernian, due to their unique background, were bigger and more successful, driving forward East of Scotland football, drawing big crowds and effectively representing the entire Irish community in Scotland, something which remained the case until the arrival of Celtic in 1888. They were starting to exert a stranglehold over Edinburgh football, something acknowledged explicitly in early Hearts history books, and tacitly by Hearts becoming so desperate to peg them back.

The second phase saw Hibernian decline, and Hearts were primed and ready to take over. From then until World War Two, Hearts were undoubtedly the bigger club; in fact, it's probably fair to say that Hearts really were the third force in Scotland in those decades, one of the few constants towards the top end of Scottish football. Aberdeen didn't start challenging at the top of Scottish football until the post-war period, and Hibernian were mediocre at best, bar the odd cup run or good season. Other clubs came and went – Motherwell, Dundee, Airdrieonians, Clyde. Those decades, from the 1890s to the 1930s, were in many ways Hearts' golden years. They were undoubtedly the team of Edinburgh. The difficulty as always was the Old Firm – and while it is tempting to point to the money-driven stranglehold they have as a consequence of modern football's structure, the period between the wars saw the Old Firm dominate as much as they ever have since.

And the third period is from World War Two to the present day, and I think it's fair to say that Hearts and Hibernian are on a par. Hibernian were resurgent after the war, and have remained a force in Scottish football ever since, as have Hearts. And there is also Aberdeen to compete with now, who are on a par with them both, and have condensed a greater level of success into a much shorter period, including, of course, two European trophies under Alex Ferguson. Aberdeen also took advantage of Rangers going bust and having to start again at the bottom in a way that the Edinburgh clubs couldn't, due to self-inflicted off-field (Hearts) and on-field (Hibernian) inadequacies.

I wrote at the outset that football history is contested, and this book's telling of the tale of the Edinburgh Derby will be as flawed as any other. So how to conclude? Well, the research, reading and conversations that have gone into creating this book have taught me a lot. I had never really considered just how fractured and difficult Hibernian's relationship with its own identity has been over the years, and how this has had an effect, ultimately, on the teams on the pitch. The flip side is the strength of Hearts' identity; to paraphrase, their sense of themselves is as strong as the old Castle Rock. That has been a strength, but I think it has also led them into trouble; such unshakeable belief in their own special place in the world has been used against them by flatterers and charlatans.

One of the difficulties with examining a rivalry is the temptation to attribute greater significance to the actions of the extreme minority than to those actions (or as is often the case, the inactions) of the majority. This is particularly true with the more controversial elements of the Edinburgh Derby, and when looking at the history of religion in Edinburgh football. In approaching this subject, I tried to keep in mind the wise words of some of Scotland's foremost academic researchers into sectarianism, Steve Bruce writing in 2004:

> The great danger of argument by illustration and anecdote is that we notice the bizarre far more than we notice the ordinary. It may be dull and worthy, but, if we are going to make assertions about large groups of people, and large-scale social processes, and even whole countries, then we need to concentrate on the typical and not the extreme.

This is always difficult when dealing with football, and not just the more controversial elements. Do Hibernian have a history of attacking football, because a couple of their two great post-war teams played brilliant attacking football for a few seasons, or are they the exception? Are Hearts the establishment team, because of their long association with Lord Rosebery? Are Hibernian supporters violent, because of the behaviour of one particular gang in the 80s and 90s? These are all valid questions.

The counter-argument is that these extremes are what make football. If we all ignored them, then football would be reduced to a bland homogenous blur. It is the differences, these extremities that make the identities and the myths – good and bad – that we all sign up to as supporters. And if we take the supporters as the constant in the life of a football club, the essence of its character and nature, the carriers of a club's DNA, then myths and stories, even if only half true – even if not true at all but widely believed – matter. Because they become true by repetition and by belief.

I have tried not to blow things out of proportion or attribute to them a significance they don't deserve – although that is obviously highly subjective. If I have got that wrong, then I apologise. But equally, in order to find the essence of a city's football, and the essence of two clubs and the rivalry that they share, I have tried to focus on some of the more interesting and, dare I say, extreme examples. They are done not to sensationalise or paint out one side as monsters and the other as angels. It is done to try and highlight the context that the Edinburgh Derby exists within.

Having grown up in Edinburgh I had a good grasp of the Edinburgh Derby, but in speaking to fans of Hibernian, Hearts, and fans of other clubs and none, I have been constantly surprised to learn new things, and uncover forgotten facts and truths. I hope that in reading this book, you have that same pleasure.

ENDNOTES

1 Salisbury Crags are rocky, vertical walls that sit beneath Arthur's Seat, an extinct volcano that towers 800 feet above the city.

2 Harris, Stuart (1920), *The Place Names of Edinburgh: their origins and history*.

3 Graham, R. (2004), *The Great Infidel: A Life of David Hume* – Birlinn, Edinburgh – p202.

4 Ibid.

5 Like Heart of Midlothian FC, this is named after Walter Scott's Waverley novels.

6 Kelly, J. & Bairner, A. (2018), 'The "talk o' the toon"? An examination of the Heart of Midlothian and Hibernian football rivalry in Edinburgh, Scotland', *Soccer and Society*, vol. 19, no. 5-6, pp. 657-672.

7 Lugton, A (1999), *The Making of Hibernian 1*. John Donald Publishers, Edinburgh.

8 John Knox was the leader of Scotland's Protestant reformation, which had begun in Edinburgh and which led to Roman Catholicism being all but wiped out, before it was reintroduced by Irish immigration (hence Irish and Catholic were used interchangeably to mean the same thing). John Knox's house on the Royal Mile is today a museum.

9 Lugton, A (1999).

10 Wilson, M. (1998), *The Hibs Story: An Official History*. Grange Communications Ltd, Edinburgh.

11 According to Hutchison & Mitchell (2018) these are Hope Street, Hope Terrace, Hope Park, Hope Park Terrace, Hope Park Crescent, Hopetoun Crescent and Hopetoun Street.

12 Despite both the Scottish national football team and both the Old Firm being in Glasgow (and all having their own stadiums), the largest sports stadium in Scotland, Murrayfield, is in Edinburgh and is the home of the Scottish Rugby Union.

13 Some of these centre around an incident when Swan, as president of the SFA, asked Celtic to remove the Irish flag from Celtic Park, a move which caused outrage and nearly forced Celtic out of Scottish football. The case was dropped when Rangers gave their rivals their support – a good example of the 'Old Firm' cartel in action.

14 There are stories that at least some 'traditional' Hibernian fans from the Cowgate did not like him, and even used to sing anti-Swan songs.

15 Kelly, J. (2019) – p6.

16 Kelly, J. (2019) – p13.

17 To this day you will see (unofficial) merchandise and supporters' flags featuring Connolly, and there is a James Connolly Hibernian Supporters' Club.

18 Kelly, J. (2007), 'Flowers of Scotland? A Sociological Analysis of National Identities, Rugby Union and Association Football in Scotland'. Doctoral thesis, University of Loughborough – p249.

19 Lugton, A (1997), *The Making of Hibernian 2: 1893–1914 The Brave Years*. John Donald Publishers, Edinburgh.

20 Ibid.

21 Kelly, J & Bairner, A (2018) 'The "talk o' the toon"? An examination of the Heart of Midlothian and Hibernian football rivalry in Edinburgh, Scotland', *Soccer and Society*, vol. 19, no. 5-6, pp. 657-672.

22 Ian Murray MP, speaking on *Remainiacs* podcast – 'So Long And Thanks For All The Fish' (24/01/2020).

23 Aberdeen have won more major trophies than either Hearts or Hibernian, and have on average done better in the league since World War Two.

24 Beaujon, A. (2018) *A Bigger Field Awaits Us: The Scottish Football Team that Fought the Great War*. Chicago Review Press: Chicago – p223.

25 Ibid, p232.

26 Ibid, p54.

27 'Hearts Lead the Way' – a poem published in the *Dundee People's Journal* on 13 March 2015, from Beaujon, A. (2018), pp23–24.

28 Auld Reekie (old smokey) is an old nickname for Edinburgh in Scots dialect.

29 *Edinburgh Evening News*, 22/04/2003.

30 MacVannan, A (2016), *We Are Hibernian*. Luath Press, Edinburgh.

31 When the Scottish Parliament was reconvened in 1999, it was located in the General Assembly for its first four years, while the new Scottish Parliament was built.

32 Finn, GPT (1994), 'Faith, hope and bigotry: Case studies of anti-Catholic prejudice in Scottish soccer and society'. In: Jarvie G, Walker G (eds), *Scottish Sport in the Making of the Nation: Ninety-Minute Patriots*. Leicester: Leicester University Press, pp. 91–112.

33 Finn (1994) p95 cited in Kelly, J. (2019).

34 Reid, W. (1924), *The Story of 'The Hearts': A Fifty Years' Retrospect 1874–1924.* The Heart of Midlothian Football Club Limited: Edinburgh – p16.

35 Bambery, C. (2014), *A People's History of Scotland.* Verso, London – p174.

36 The Masons, in the context of Scottish football were/ are perceived as a bastion of Protestantism and are often associated with conspiracies within Scottish football (it was a running joke that referees were Masons, for example) – although it's the Catholic Church that bans Catholics from also being Masons – the end result is the same, a Protestant-only secret society. It should be noted that the Masons aren't discriminatory when it comes to the religion of their members.

37 East Fife currently play in the fourth tier of the Scottish league in front of average crowds of 800.

38 Clyde moved out of Glasgow to the town of Cumbernauld and currently play in the fourth tier, in front of average crowds of 900.

39 This was the precursor to the League Cup, but didn't include Aberdeen due to wartime restrictions on travel until its final iteration in 1945/46. Rangers won it four times (1940/41 (defeating Hearts in the final), 1941/42, 1942/43 and 1944/45, with Hibernian (1943/44) and Aberdeen (1945/46) the other winners.

40 They remain one of only two, with Alex Ferguson's Aberdeen team of the 1980s matching it in 1983/84 and 1984/85.

41 In Hibs' official club song dating from the early 1960s, 'Glory Glory to the Hibees', there is a line 'against the famous English clubs, we're better than the rest'.

42 This includes two 'floodlight friendlies' – matches held to open their respective floodlights. The matches were won one apiece. Despite being friendlies both matches drew crowds of 25,000 (no doubt a large novelty factor helped with this).

43 The Rex Kingsley Footballer of the Year award is a good measure of how pluralistic Scottish football was in those post-war years, with players from 11 different clubs receiving the award during its 14-year history, including from Partick Thistle, Raith Rovers, Falkirk, Clyde, Kilmarnock, Dundee and Motherwell, as well as Rangers (twice), Hearts (twice), Hibernian and Celtic.

44 A minor competition played early in the season during the 1970s for the highest-scoring teams, but also a way for a major corporate sponsor to get around the SFA's ban on commercial sponsors for the Scottish Cup

45 Given Celtic's frequent European commitments at this time, it's doubtful they took the competition entirely seriously.

46 Celtic won the European Cup in 1967 (and were surprisingly beaten in the final in 1970 by Feyenoord), as well as nine titles in a row in this era; and Rangers, while not as strong, still managed to win the European Cup Winners' Cup in 1972.

47 'New Firm' was a media nickname applied to Aberdeen and Dundee United in the early to mid-1980s, which reflected their rise to prominence in Scottish football, upturning the previous established order.

48 Dundee United also reached the UEFA Cup Final in 1986/87, and the European Cup semi-final in 1983/84.

49 There were two further defeats in minor tournaments, but by this period the local trophies had lost their appeal.

50 Price, N. (1997), *Gritty, Gallant, Glorious: A History and Complete Record of The Hearts 1946–1997*, p96.

51 The other winners were Berwick Rangers (2), Mossend Swifts (2), Bo'ness (1), St Bernard's (1), Leith Athletic (1), Edinburgh Thistle (1), University of Edinburgh (1) and 3rd Edinburgh Rifle Volunteers (1). Since it became a reserve/youth fixture, Hibernian have won it 14 times, Hearts seven times.

52 Ironically, just a year later Dundee tried to buy over Dundee United, their owner citing Mercer as an example to follow. The fact that Dundee, also the traditional 'establishment' team, and Dundee United (called Dundee Hibernian until 1923) had sprung from Dundee's large Irish community is also striking. Anyone who knows Scottish football can imagine what the response of Dundee United manager (and chairman) Jim McLean would have been!

53 'The talk of the toun [town] are the boys in maroon' is a line from the Hearts club song.

54 Aberdeen have never developed Pittodrie the way that Hibernian and Hearts have done, and despite exploring options To move to a new stadium, it has never materialised. This has undoubtedly given them a financial edge at various times.

55 Eoin Jess was a breakout young star with Aberdeen in the early 1990s, when the club were still riding the end of the Ferguson-era wave of success. His early promise was never fulfilled, partly as a result of serious injuries.

56 It's worth remembering that this was pre-2008 banking crisis, when Edinburgh's banking sector was at its peak and home to some of the largest financial companies and banks in the world – not some immature, easy-to-crack banking market.

57 *Always the Bridesmaid* was the name of a Hearts fanzine in the 1980s.

58 Since World War Two, Aberdeen have won four league titles (third best), seven Scottish Cups (third best), six League Cups (third best) and of course won the European Cup Winners' Cup and the European Super Cup (second best).

59 From season 1946/47 until the end of season 2022/23.

60 'Hearts to stay at Tynecastle and increase capacity of stadium' – BBC website, 03/12/2015.

BIBLIOGRAPHY

Aitken, M & Mercer, W (1988) *Heart to Heart: The Anatomy of a Football Club.* Mainstream Publishing, Edinburgh

Allan, J (1923) *The Story of the Rangers: Fifty Years' Football 1873-1923 A Jubilee History.* Rangers Football Club

Bambery, C (2014) *A People's History of Scotland.* Verso Publishing, London

Beaujon, A (2018) *A Bigger Field Awaits Us: The Scottish Football Team that Fought the Great War.* Chicago Review Press, Chicago

Bell, T (2019) *Choose Life. Choose Leith: Trainspotting on Location.* Luath Press, Edinburgh

Bruce, S., Glendinning, T., Paterson, I., Rosie, M (2004) *Sectarianism in Scotland.* Edinburgh University Press, Edinburgh

Burns, S (2017) *It's not all about the Old Firm: Defying the odds in Scottish football.* Pitch Publishing, Worthing

Campbell, J (2011) *At Easter Road they Play: A post-war history of Hibs volume one 1945-1967.* Birlinn Publishing, Edinburgh

Campbell, T & Woods, P (1986) *The Glory and the Dream: The History of Celtic F.C. 1887-1986.* Mainstream Publishing, Edinburgh

Colquhoun, I (2016) *From Oblivion to Hampden: Hibs Heroes of 1991.* Pitch Publishing, Worthing

Coogan, T.P. (2000) *Wherever Green is Worn: The Story of the Irish Diaspora.* Random House, London

Dishon, P.D. (2012) *The Delaneys of Edinburgh.* Grosvenor House Publishing, Guildford

Docherty, G & Thomson, P (1975) *100 Years of Hibs 1875-1975.* John Donald Publishers, Edinburgh

Donaldson, M (2006) *Believe! Hearts, from turmoil to triumph at Tynecastle.* Mainstream Publishing, Edinburgh

Donovan, M (2021) *Dave Mackay – Football's Braveheart.* Pitch Publishing, Worthing

Dykes, D & Colvin, A (2007) *These Colours Don't Run: Inside the Hibs Capital City Service.* Fort Publishing, Ayr

Fairgrieve, J (1986) *The Boys in Maroon: The Authorised Inside Story of an Unforgettable Season.* Mainstream Publishing, Edinburgh

Flint, J & Kelly, J (2013) *Bigotry, Football and Scotland.* Edinburgh University Press, Edinburgh

Fraser, W.H. (2000) *Scottish Popular Politics.* Polygon Publishing, Edinburgh

Fry, M (2009) *Edinburgh: A History of the City.* Macmillan, London

Gallagher, T (1987) *Edinburgh Divided: John Cormack and No Popery in the 1930s.* Polygon Publishing, Edinburgh

Graham, R (2006) *The Great Infidel: A Life of David Hume.* Birlinn, Edinburgh

Harvie, C (2002) *Scotland: A Short History.* Oxford University Press, Oxford

Hepburn, R (1990) *Ten of Hearts: The Heart of Midlothian Story 1980-1990.* Mainstream Publishing, Edinburgh

Holmes, R (2020) *Forgotten: Scotland's Former Football League Clubs.* Self-published history

Hutchison, J & Mitchell, A (2018) *1824 – The World's First Foot-Ball Club: John Hope and the Edinburgh footballers, a story of sport, education and philanthropy* – Andy Mitchell Media, Dunblane

Kelly, J & Bairner, A (2018) *The 'talk o' the toon'? An examination of the Heart of Midlothian and Hibernian football rivalry in Edinburgh, Scotland.* Soccer and Society, vol. 19, no. 5-6, pp. 657-672.

Kelly, John (2019). *Flowers of Scotland?: A Sociological Analysis of National Identities, Rugby Union and Association Football in Scotland.* figshare. https://hdl.handle.net/2134/7977.

Lee, C (2021) *Origin Stories: The Pioneers Who Took Football to the World.* Pitch Publishing, Worthing

Lownie, R (2004) *Auld Reekie: An Edinburgh Anthology.* Mainstream Publishing, Edinburgh

Lugton, A (1995) *The Making of Hibernian.* John Donald Publishers, Edinburgh

Lugton, A (1997) *The Making of Hibernian 2: 1893–1914 The Brave Years.* John Donald Publishers, Edinburgh

Lugton, A (1998) *The Making of Hibernian 3: 1914–1946 The Romantic Years.* John Donald Publishers, Edinburgh

Mackie, A (1959) *The Hearts: The Story of Heart of Midlothian F.C.* Stanley Paul & Co, London

Mackay, J.R. (1995) *Hibernian: The Easter Road Story.* John Donald Publishers, Edinburgh

Mackay, J.R. (1986) *The Hibees: The Story of Hibernian Football Club.* John Donald Publishers, Edinburgh

Mackay, J.R. (1990) *Hibernian: The Complete Story.* John Donald Publishers, Edinburgh

MacVannan, A (2016) *We Are Hibernian: Scottish Cup Winners 2016.* Luath Press Limited, Edinburgh

Mark, B (1994) *Hibernian FC: The War Years 1939-1946.* Archways Promotions, Edinburgh

Murray, I (2019) *This Is Our Story: How the fans kept their Hearts beating.* Luath Press Limited, Edinburgh

Niven, D (2021) *Pride of the Hearts*. Corkerhill Press

Park, G (2008) *St Bernard's Football Club or when the well ran dry!* Self-published history by George H Park

Pogorzelski, K. (2023) *Divided Cities: The World's Most Passionate Single City Derbies*. Pitch Publishing, Chichester

Rafferty, J (1973) *One Hundred Years of Scottish Football*. Pan Books, London

Price, N (1997) *Gritty, Gallant, Glorious: A history and complete record of the Hearts 1946-1997*. Norrie Price Publishing

Purdie, T (2014) *Hearts at War 1914-1918*. Amberley Publishing, Stroud

Purdie, T (2012) *Hearts: The Golden Years*. Amberley Publishing, Stroud

Reid, W (1924) *The Story of the Hearts: A Fifty Years' Retrospect 1874-1924*. Heart of Midlothian Football Club, Edinburgh

Robertson, J (2022) *Robbo: My autobiography*. Black & White Publishing, Edinburgh

Scott, B (1988) *Hearts Greats*. John Donald Publishers, Edinburgh

Smith, M (2012) *Hearts Greatest Games*. Pitch Publishing, Worthing

Smith, M (2018) *The Team for Me. Fifty Years of Following Hearts*. Pitch Publishing, Worthing

Smith, A (2005) *Heartfelt: Supping Bovril from the Devil's Cup*. Birlinn, Edinburgh

Smith, C.J. (1986) *Historic South Edinburgh*. Charles Skilton Ltd, Haddington

Stanton, P & Pia, S (1989) *The Quiet Man*. Sportsprint / John Donald Publishing, Edinburgh

Stephen, J (2018) *What Kept You, Hibs? How Hibernian FC Turned Disaster Into Triumph and Ended Football's Greatest Curse.* Saughton Drum Publishing, Edinburgh

Stevenson, R.L. (first published 1887) *Edinburgh: Picturesque Notes*

Stevenson, R.L. (first published 1886) *The Strange Case of Dr Jekyll and Mr Hyde.* London

Turnbull, E & Hannan, M (2006) *Eddie Turnbull: Having A Ball.* Mainstream Publishing, Edinburgh

Valentine, D.S. (2006) *Leith at Random.* Porthole Publications, Edinburgh

Watson, C. (2005) *The Battle for Hearts and Minds: Changing fortunes at Heart of Midlothian Football Club.* Black and White Publishing, Edinburgh

Weddell, S (2015) *A Tale of Two Season: The Fall and Rise of Heart of Midlothian.* Pitch Publishing, Worthing

Wilkie, J (1984) *Across the Great Divide: A history of professional football in Dundee.* Mainstream Publishing, Edinburgh

Wilson, M (1998) *The Hibs Story: An Official History.* Grange Communications Ltd, Edinburgh

Wilson, B (2017) *Celtic: The Official History.* Arena Publishing, Edinburgh

Wilson, R (2012) *Inside the Divide: One City, Two Teams, The Old Firm.* Canongate Books, Edinburgh

Wright, T (2017) *Hibernian: The Life and Times of a Famous Football Club.* Luath Press Limited, Edinburgh

Wright, T (2010) *The Golden Years: Hibernian in the days of the Famous Five.* The Derby Book Publishing Company, Derby

Wright, T (2011) *Hibernian: From Joe Baker to Turnbull's Tornadoes.* Luath Press Limited, Edinburgh